Divorcing & Healing from a Narcissistic Man

A Practical Woman's Guide to Recovery from the Hidden Emotional and Psychological Abuse of a Destructive Marriage to a Narcissistic Man

By

Dr. Isabel Meredith Brown

© **Copyright 2020 - All rights reserved.**

The content contained within this book may not be reproduced, duplicated or transmitted without direct written permission from the author or the publisher.

Under no circumstances will any blame or legal responsibility be held against the publisher, or author, for any damages, reparation, or monetary loss due to the information contained within this book. Either directly or indirectly.

Legal Notice:
This book is copyright protected. This book is only for personal use. You cannot amend, distribute, sell, use, quote or paraphrase any part, or the content within this book, without the consent of the author or publisher.

Disclaimer Notice:
Please note the information contained within this document is for educational and entertainment purposes only. All effort has been executed to present accurate, up to date, and reliable, complete information. No warranties of any kind are declared or implied. Readers acknowledge that the author is not engaging in the rendering of legal, financial, medical or professional advice. The content within this book has been derived from various sources. Please consult a licensed professional before attempting any techniques outlined in this book.

By reading this document, the reader agrees that under no circumstances is the author responsible for any losses, direct or indirect, which are incurred as a result of the use of information contained within this document, including, but not limited to, errors, omissions, or inaccuracies.

Table of Contents

Introduction 8
   You Are Not Alone 9
   You Deserve Better 10
   What You Will Learn from Reading This Book 13

Chapter 1   Understanding Narcissism 16
   What is a Narcissist? 21
   Types of Narcissism 23
   The Traits of a Narcissist 24
   Are People Born Narcissistic? 27
   How Did You Fall for A Narcissist? 30

Chapter 2   Marriage with a Narcissist 34
   The Overvaluation Phase 35
   The Devaluation Phase 38
   The Discard Phase 43
   The Healing Phase 44
   Move on and focus on you. 45
   Why Did I Marry a Narcissist? 45

Chapter 3   Divorcing a Narcissist 49
   Why it is Difficult to Divorce a Narcissist 51
   How a Trauma Bond Develops 52
   Stages of a Narcissist Trauma Bond Formation 53
   Symptoms That a Person Suffers from a Narcissistic Trauma Bond
.... 56

Tactics for Dealing with and Severing a Narcissistic Trauma Bond 57

The Best Practices for Getting through a Divorce from a Narcissist as Unscathed as Possible 61

The Benefits of Divorcing a Narcissistic Husband 64

Chapter 4   Super Techniques and Power-ups for Recovery after a Narcissistic Marriage 68

Technique 1 – Seize Contact with the Narcissist 68

Technique 2 – Reclaim Responsibility for Your Life 72

Powerful Ways in Which You Can Develop and Strengthen Your Intuition 77

Technique 3 – Release the Trauma You Suffered Back into the Universe 80

Technique 4 – Ensure That another Narcissist Does Not Take Advantage of You 87

Chapter 5   How to Heal from the Emotional Trauma 98

Reinvent yourself 98

What is PTSD? 99

The Signs and Symptoms of PTSD 101

Being Diagnosed with PTSD 103

How Victims of Narcissistic Abuse Develop PTSD 103

Why Healing from Trauma or PTSD Triggered by Narcissistic Abuse Is Different 105

Healing from Trauma or PTSD from Narcissistic Abuse 107

Chapter 6   Discover Your True Worth 117

Work on Your Self-Image 124

Be Proud of the Fact That You Are a Survivor of Narcissistic Abuse 126
Use the Power of Visualization 127
Start Acknowledging and Celebrating Your Accomplishments ... 128

Conclusion 130
Forgive but Never Forget 130
Final Thoughts 133

More Books by the Author 142

Introduction

You feel wounded, don't you? The scars may not be visible to other people, but being in a relationship with a narcissist is comparable to being kicked where it hurts the most - your heart – and the path to healing is not straight or clear. This person made living a burden. He picked at your clothes. Or maybe he verbally put you down? Threatened you with violence, perhaps?

He tore you down piece by piece and putting the pieces back together can seem impossible, especially when the wounds are still fresh. It may feel like no one understands what you are going through, and no one may ever to a certain extent. Your outlook on life and how you view yourself has been changed forever. The motives of other people may seem suspicious because you now know that a person's initial charismatic persona may turn into a deadly trap. Thus, your social interactions suffer and you develop trust issues. Your work performance and your relationships with other people such as friends, family, and colleagues, have suffered, too. This relationship with this one person has impacted your entire life and, most importantly, it has changed you mentally and emotionally forever. This relationship may have even changed you physically.

Have you admitted it to yourself yet? That you were abused by this person? Do you recognize the signs of this abuse? It does not just have to be physical, especially when the tools of abuse that a narcissist uses are often invisible. The verbal jabs both subtle and obvious, the smirk that leaves you doubting yourself, the constant letdowns that make you neglect your health in all ways, the looks that have the power to drain you emotionally…

The signs are wide and varied, but the fact is this man did indeed abuse you. The first step to putting that abuse in the past where it belongs is admitting to yourself that you were this man's victim. The start of something is the most difficult part, but you can do it. I have faith in you, and this book was written to help you get to the mental and emotional space where you have that same faith in yourself.

You Are Not Alone

You may be wondering how I know so much about you when we have not met, and the answer is that I have met many other women who have gone through a similar situation to you – surviving a relationship with a narcissistic male partner. These women too found it difficult to come to grips with the brutal reality that they had gone through. They too had periods of hopelessness and could not fathom how they would move past this trauma. They also found the strength to put one foot in front of the other to take that first step, then the next one that road to recovery. And you can do the same.

How do I know you can do it? I know because of one indisputable fact – you are a woman and have unimaginable power held within your body. You have the power to create life. You are able to bleed every month and still function. You are able to singularly run a household. You are able to nurture others and provide comfort in an effortless way that others cannot.

This man is nothing compared to the power you wield even if he has managed to convince you otherwise.

You Deserve Better

You have read this far into this book and that allows me to assume that either you are a woman who is currently in a narcissistic relationship and wants to know how to get out or you are someone who has already got an out of a narcissistic relationship and wants to know how she can heal to move on from this life of abuse. The first thing I want to do is congratulate you for realizing that this is an unhealthy situation and also realizing that there is a need to get out. Many women in narcissistic relationships never reach that point and live a life filled with this abuse or, more, unfortunately, do not live to tell their story.

This book was written to give you your power back. You deserve more than this man has dished out to you. You deserve more than to be controlled and isolated. You deserve to be happy and healthy rather than constantly worrying about someone else's disregard for your personal boundaries for their own personal gain and selfish needs.

A narcissist is a skilled manipulator and he may have convinced you that you deserve nothing more than to be someone's doormat but this is far from true. You deserve the best and that includes in your romantic relationships. You deserve someone who makes you feel secure and empowered. You deserve someone that helps you build your self-worth and self-esteem. Anything less is beneath you and this book was written to help you realize that truth. I will keep on reinstating that fact in this introduction and the chapters to come because I want to drill it into your head until you a solidified in the authenticity of this statement - you deserve the best and taking abuse from a narcissistic man is far beneath you.

After being abused by a narcissist, this may be a truth that is hard for you to believe. Do not worry if you do not believe me now. I understand that you may feel inadequate and lost. You may even be on the brink of giving up. But you have not and that is the most important thing.

Healing after being in a narcissistic relationship takes time and it takes your dedication. These are the ingredients that make it possible for you to heal and claim the things that you deserve out of life and out of a romantic relationship. Making a full recovery after such a failed relationship is possible and that possibility lies in the power of your resilience as a woman.

I have witnessed other women do it and have been amazed by the power of being female. My words to offer you assistance in your recovery are not empty promises. Not only have I witnessed other females recover from a narcissistic relationship, but I also have years of experience and study in this field as a doctor. My job is to help women recover from abusive relationships and I take my job seriously.

I have helped many women implement the tips and techniques for recovery that I will outline in the chapters to come. I have seen these women implement these strategies in their own lives to see the massive results. I have seen the power of a woman's dedication to recovery and how it has allowed her to grab onto new hope and pave the way to a new life for herself after such a traumatic experience. These women can do it and you can do it, too. And the sooner you take action, the better off you will be.

Just imagine a future where you are not suffering injustice at the hands of a man who is only empowered by a wrong sense of entitlement. Imagine steering your life in the direction you want rather than being on the path that is decided by someone who does not have a true claim on taking that control from you. Imagine being happy and content with the woman that you are.

Just imagine... Then believe that those images are a future that you can create for yourself. Remember, you deserve that future, so work toward turning it into fruition. Your effort is the only way it will become a reality. I cannot do it for you no matter how much I would like to ease your burden and neither can anyone else. You have to pull up your big girl panties on and get this done ASAP!

What You Will Learn from Reading This Book

There will be no beating around the bush in this book. This will be a frank, no-holds-barred detail of strategies you can use to empower yourself and no longer be a victim to a man who is careless with something as precious as you are. I did not pull these strategies out of a hat nor conjure them by another form of magic. These strategies are backed by science and proven by years of research as well as results that other women have gained from using them.

As a result, I can promise you that you will gain value from every single page to come. I will educate you on the following:

- What a narcissist is and narcissistic traits that this person carries
- How to tell if you are in a narcissistic relationship
- Why and how women from all backgrounds fall for narcissistic men
- The phases of a narcissistic relationship
- Why it is hard to end a relationship with a narcissist
- How to heal from the trauma of a narcissistic relationship with practical tips and solutions

- How to discover your true worth and rebuild your self-esteem
- How to set healthy boundaries so that your future romantic relationships will be different
- Much more!

Healing and personal recovery of any kind are difficult processes. I will continue to reinstate that it is possible to recover from a narcissistic relationship no matter how much damage this relationship has done. However, I will not sugarcoat the fact that this is a hard road to travel, especially since this is an individualized process that can only be traveled by you. There will be potholes, twists and turns, unexpected storms, and events that pop out of nowhere.

The silver lining is that no matter how toilsome of a journey you may have, the end result is more than worth the effort. It is that you will have new hope in your life. It means that you will be able to restore and build your confidence, change your entire perspective of yourself and other people, and build boundaries that allow you to spot narcissists in the future, so you can avoid them, and build healthy relationships with people that want the best for you. After you have traveled that road, you will be able to proudly proclaim that you are a survivor and no longer anyone's victim.

I implore you to not just read this book as a pastime. This book needs to be read with a frame of mind that leads to action. You need to put yourself in the driver's seat of your life so that you can reclaim it boldly. You are a woman and that roar of yours is powerful even after you have been temporarily beaten by someone else. Use the information in the following pages to take action with the frame of mind to empower yourself so that your future is brighter, healthier, happier, and more fulfilled.

Thank you for downloading this book. I wish you the best of luck in getting past this hurdle in your life because I have faith that you will not only survive this stage of your life, but you will thrive after it. Turn the page to reclaim the beautiful person you have always been!

Chapter 1

Understanding Narcissism

Let me tell you a true story.

There was a young woman. For the sake of confidentiality, we will call this woman Rosa. She had everything going for her. She had just graduated from college and was on the fast track to attaining her career goals. She had just moved out of her parents' place, both of whom were supportive of the path that she had set for her life. She had a supportive group of friends and healthy social relationships. This woman was motivated, inspired, confident, and thought that nothing could take her off the fast track to achieving her goals and dreams.

Then Rosa met the man we will call Tim. He was tall, dark and handsome – like a hero that had fallen straight out a romance novel. He had approached her with intense eyes, words that wrapped around her like silk, and passion she had never felt directed at her before. Tim made Rosa feel like she was the only woman in the world in just an instant.

He showered her with compliments and praise. She woke up to his *Good morning, beautiful* texts, and would have a smile on her face for the rest of the day. She went to sleep only after she absolutely could not keep her eyes open because she was talking to Tim on the phone.

Tim was relentless in his pursuit of this unsuspecting young woman and soon they progressed passed the talking phase and were actively dating. The first time they made love was beautiful. The way he had been attentive to her needs had made her realize that she had fallen in love. He told her he loved her, too. He told her she was the only one for him and that he wanted to marry her. She believed him. He seemed so sincere that she could not possibly believe otherwise.

Tim was not perfect, even though Rosa would describe him as such if anyone asked. Sometimes he drank a little too much and yelled at her and there were a few times he would citizen her outfit. But those were things Rosa overlooked. So what if he had a few flaws? Everyone did.

So Rosa moved into Tim's apartment when he asked, despite the concerns her friends and family expressed. She got his name tattooed on her arm even though that was something she swore she would never do. She allowed him to make love to her without protection because he said it would make their love stronger even though she knew better. She did not hesitate to say yes when he asked for her hand in marriage and she wore the ring proudly. They eloped because Tim convinced her that anyone that did not wish them well should not be part of their wedding even though Rosa had dreamed of a big wedding as a little girl.

The two people were in their own little world and it seemed like nothing could tear them apart even though only a few weeks had passed. It was fast Rosa knew, but love was not bound by time. Their love story seemed a fairy tale until it was not.

The red flags started to pop up just a few days after their union was official and they left Rosa confused.

At first, it was small things. Tim would chastise her for the way she dressed, talked, and ate. The words were more brutal than those he used when they dated. He said it was because he just wanted her to be the best version of herself that she could be. So, she listened and adjusted to his sayings. Then he started to lose his temper and shout at her. But then he convinced her it was just because he was under so much pressure at work. So, she forgave him and even started to blame herself for the episodes. If she had not done this or that, he would not have acted out that way, right?

Then he started becoming upset when she talked to other people on the phone, especially other men. It did not matter if they were friends, family or colleagues, he would have a fit. But that was normal. Any man as in love with her like Tim would be overprotective and jealous. That was what Tim said and when he doted on her, she believed that this was just a mild side effect of his strong feelings for her.

So she adjusted her behavior and adjusted some more every time he complained about what she did and did not do, about how she dressed and talked, about the times that she came in and the places she went, about the people she spent time with... The love that had placed Rosa on a high now weighed her down.

Still, she stayed and even hid her unhappiness from the people in her life. She isolated herself from them and her life became a monotonous routine of work and spending time in the apartment even when Tim was out, which became increasingly frequent. He told her she was crazy to believe that he was unfaithful, even when he came home smelling of alcohol and another woman's perfume.

When Rosa found out that she was pregnant, she thought this would be the news that would make things go back to the way they had been at the start of the relationship. The news had the opposite effect though, and the couple seemed to argue daily, which usually resulted in Rosa breaking down into tears and Tim storming out of the apartment. Then he would return with flowers and her favorite chocolates to tell her he loves her still. When he gave her *that* look, she would believe him.

Their relationship became a tale of extremes. There were intense fights, then bouts of loving behavior that almost convinced Rosa that she was hallucinating the bad parts. But the scales tipped until it was mostly bad times, which was quite stressful and made her pregnancy difficult.

She did not know when it started but somewhere along the way, she convinced herself that she was the cause of the troubles in the relationship. This was especially true when she confirmed that Tim was indeed seeing other women and blamed her inferiority as a woman as the reason. She could not help but think that it was true.

Rosa almost convinced herself to leave a few times, but there was a pull that made her stay. It was as if Tim sensed her building resolved during these times and then he would transform back into the man she knew when they first met. He would convince her that they could be a happy family and raise their baby in a stable home with two loving parents. She would be convinced that this would the last time that she would forgive his derogatory name-calling and words but it never was.

Then one day, their verbal argument escalated and Tim hit her. It was enough to send her reeling across the room. She fell and landed hard. Darkness claimed Rosa's vision for some time, but when she regained consciousness, there was blood gushing from between her legs and she had been abandoned by the man she had married.

Tim's abuse landed Rosa in the hospital and she lost her baby. That was the wakeup call the woman needed. Tim was arrested the next day and Rosa filed for divorce. Even though she is free of that man today, the experience at this man's hand left her changed forever.

Rosa was manipulated into believing she fell in love but in the end, she never truly knew the man she thought was the one. She had been completely fooled by the façade he presented and she paid dearly for the fact.

Rosa is a woman I have counseled and while she has come a long way since the day she entered my office, she still continues to suffer symptoms of PTSD. She did not realize it at the time, but she was the victim of a narcissistic relationship with a narcissistic man.

Rosa is not alone. There are almost 20 million people with narcissistic tendencies in the United States alone and 75% of that number is men. The kicker is that most of these men do not realize that they have a problem and continue to victimize other people with complete disregard for the hurt and devastation they cause.

What is a Narcissist?

The formal definition of narcissism is that it is a personality disorder whereby a person displays an inflated sense of importance and a lack of empathy towards others, yet still has an excessive need for attention and admiration from other people. My definition is far simpler to understand. A narcissist is a pompous, attention-seeking individual who does not care about anyone else because they lack the ability to.

Narcissism is a spectrum disorder. People can display varying levels and intensities of the disorder and to some extent, everyone displays narcissistic tendencies. It is when these behaviors become consistent and affect relationships, that it gets described as narcissism.

Narcissistic people typically come across as extremely confident with a shallow glance, but this just masks a fragile sense of self-esteem that can be easily bruised at the slightest negative feedback or criticism. True confidence does not need validation or attention from others, but this is exactly what a narcissist needs. Narcissists need other people to recognize their accomplishments and their person to feel special, wanted, and validated. This can lead to excessive bragging.

As a result of this need for validation, narcissists feel the need to win at everything, even if they do not put in true effort. They fantasize about being the best such as being the most powerful, successful, beautiful, and accomplished in the crowd. They need to make these fantasies become reality and as such, only associate with people that can help them fulfill their fantasies. Still, with these associations, they do not want to be outshined by anyone else or else, they perceive this as a threat.

As a result of the above-stated personality traits, people with narcissistic personality disorder are unhappy for the most part because without special treatment, they feel worthless.

This leads to unbalanced relationships where they are the takers who rarely give and only give with the intention of receiving more.

Narcissism borders into psychopathy when the narcissist has a total disregard for moral behavior and does not feel any type of remorse for his or her actions.

Types of Narcissism

The first type of narcissism is called grandiose narcissism. This type of narcissist displays high levels of grandiosity, dominance, and aggression. These are the type of narcissists that portray a high level of outward confidence and have a tendency to overstate their capabilities.

This type of narcissism often develops due to this person being treated as if they are superior to others in their childhood. They grow up with the expectation that this type of treatment will continue indefinitely and act in a way that is fitting with that expectation. These types of narcissists are highly unlikely to remain faithful in their romantic relationships and are quick to leave when they feel that romantic relationships do not cater to their inflated sense of superiority.

On the other hand, vulnerable narcissism displays more emotional sensitivity because this serves as a protection mechanism for feelings of incompetence or inadequacy. This type of narcissist displays entitlement issues, anxiety, and often plays the victim when they think that they do not get the treatment that they deserve.

This is because this type of narcissism yo-yos between feeling inferior and superior to other people. Again, this type of narcissism often develops because of childhood issues. This development is for a different reason, though. The development of vulnerable narcissism has been often a coping mechanism for abuse or neglect from adult influences. This makes vulnerable narcissists easily jealous, possessive, volatile, and paranoid, red flags for any romantic relationship.

The Traits of a Narcissist

Narcissism can only be officially diagnosed by a licensed medical professional. To be officially diagnosed with narcissistic personality disorder, a person has to display these criteria:

- Being preoccupied with fantasies of gaining excessive amounts of power, beauty, success, or love.
- Needing an excessive amount of admiration and attention from other people.
- Needing to be envied by others or believing that others are envious of them.
- Displaying an exaggerated sense of self-importance.
- Having a deep-seated belief that he or she is unique and special in a way that only special or high-status persons can understand.
- Partaking in exploitative behavior.
- Lacking empathy.
- Displaying arrogant behaviors or attitudes.

These traits can manifest themselves in a variety of ways such as:

- Being extremely charming at the beginning of a relationship. This is what makes it so easy for a woman to fall for a narcissistic partner. The narcissist engages in love bombing, which is a way

of influencing a person's feelings by demonstrating large amounts of affection and attention. This results in large amounts of compliments and doting so that the other person becomes used to the attention and, therefore, more susceptible to giving the narcissist the things that they require out of that relationship.
- Hogging conversations with constant talk about their accomplishments and achievements. This is a result of the narcissist's needing to be admired and have the attention focused on them. Conversations will, therefore, have lots of name dropping and filled with links to influential people because the narcissist needs to be seen as an important individual.
- Insisting on having the best of everything like the best-looking house on the street, the most beautiful romantic partner, or having the best outfit at an event. This stems from the narcissist's need to portray their sense of superiority.
- Expecting special treatment and automatic compliance of their desires from other people. The narcissist feels that the world revolves around them and so places their needs and wants above other people's own.
- Not having many long-term friendships. Narcissists only maintain the charming behavior and attitude for the short-term. Therefore, they do not form deep connections with other people often. As a result, their longer term relationships most

commonly consist of casual acquaintances, people that they can bash other people with, and enemies.
- Frequently belittling others, they perceive beneath them. This behavior is a pit to reinstate their sense of superiority.
- They believe that they are right all the time and never apologizes. A narcissist is not good at compromising and, therefore, does not see disagreements as disagreements. Rather, they see them as an opportunity to teach another person their truth. As a result, the narcissist will not take responsibility in situations where they will be seen in a negative light. They will blame others, instead.
- They react in an exaggerated manner if someone breaks up with them. The narcissist likes to be on the controlling end of things. Therefore, they do not take being broken up with well. They will make it difficult for the other person to break the romantic connection until they find someone else they think is more valuable of their time and energy.
- Being manipulative and controlling in relationships. No tactic is beneath this person in order to get what they want and manipulation and control are common techniques to accomplish this.

It is very easy for narcissistic persons to feel slighted if any of the conditions that they feel that they are entitled to are not met. Because they secretly have feelings of shame, insecurity, low confidence, and vulnerability, it is very easy for this person to feel slighted. As a result, they do not handle any form of criticism, whether it is well-intentioned or not, well.

Narcissists do not handle change well either because they need to feel as if they are in control at all times. Therefore, they often react with rage and contempt when change happens or someone disagrees with their ways of doing things. Narcissists have difficulty regulating their emotions and vengeful behavior is common as well as the use of underhanded tactics to get back at people or get their way.

It is not uncommon for a narcissistic person to suffer from mood and mental disorders like depression and anxiety because they have this expectation of perfection from themselves and other people, and as we all know, perfection is not an attainable state.

Are People Born Narcissistic?

Narcissists are made, not born even though the traits can show up pretty early in a person's life. The type of narcissism that develops due to a toddler's experience is called malignant narcissism. Unfortunately, a lot of toddlers are neglected by their parents or guardians and, therefore, do not have the support they need to develop healthily during this stage. This underdevelopment is something that flows into adulthood.

As toddlers, we think we are the center of the universe. This is quite normal because this is simply a developmental stage. It is with our parents and guardians' assistance that we learn the need for implementing and enforcing our personal boundaries and how to respect the boundaries of other people. With this learning comes the throwing of tantrums, experimenting with manipulation techniques, and having unreasonable expectations that can lead to a host of behaviors like crying and hitting. This developmental stage is commonly known as the terrible twos, which is not just limited to the age of two years old. Some children need more time to get past this stage, even with healthy adult guidance.

If a child is not sufficiently aided during this stage, then he or she fails to properly learn to respect personal boundaries and grows up thinking that the world really does revolve around their wants and needs. As a result, this person will have the same reactions of a toddler to not having their desires met such as tantrum-throwing and having unrealistic expectations of other people as an adult. While we can tolerate or even watch on fondly as a child has a tantrum, this is not the same for when an adult does it because it can become irritating and even dangerous. Imagine a 200-pound man throwing furniture and kicking the walls because he did not get what he wanted and you know what I mean.

This inadequate leadership through this development stage in toddlerhood is the reason why children of narcissists typically also become narcissists. Narcissists do not know how to teach anyone how to be empathetic or how to respect boundaries because they are not capable. They do not know how to teach a person how to stop doing things to seek attention because attention-seeking is part of their personality. A narcissist cannot teach anyone else how to value the opinion of others and listen to other people's needs and wants. Therefore, they will teach a child to take on their apathetic tendencies and so the cycle repeats itself.

Therefore, the development of narcissism is largely based on genetics and the environment a child is exposed to. Neglect is not the only reason that a child can develop narcissism. Other environmental factors such as excessive criticism, abuse of any kind, insensitive parents, being over-praised, and excessive pampering are also common contributions to the development of the disorder.

Another contribution to the development of narcissism is abnormalities in the genes that play a role in the development of behavior. This simply means that the brains of narcissists may be wired differently than other people's brains and as such, this is reflected in their behavior.

Even though some children already display narcissistic tendencies early, most often the disorder develops in a person's teens and early adulthood. Narcissism is a prevalent disorder because narcissistic people do not recognize that they have a problem that needs fixing. Therefore, they do nothing to change their behavior and can even make it worse by indulging in escapist activities like doing drugs and excessive alcohol.

Even when some narcissists recognize that they have a problem, they hesitate to seek help because that would be a blow to their already fragile self-esteem as this would be seen as a mark of imperfection.

How Did You Fall for A Narcissist?

The person described above sounds horrible, so this begs the question of why and how anyone would gain feelings for such an individual. There must be something wrong with people who do it, right? That is incorrect.

Narcissists target their victims. They do not go after just anyone. People who are honest, compassionate, authentic, and empathetic are prime victims of narcissists because they can feed off these people's nurturing and loving energies. There is nothing that you did to attract this person. This person sought you out and deliberately hid their true colors from you. <u>Narcissists are like chameleons. They change their colors to suit the environment so that they can gain as much benefit from the people and situations they encounter.</u> This person knows that they cannot reveal their true colors upfront and needs to plot and scheme to get into relationships that gain them the highest values.

Women get into relationships with narcissistic men because these men strive to make a great first impression and hold this façade until they have thoroughly hooked these women. They study these women to learn their needs and wants out of a partner, then adjust their behavior to fit those criteria. They typically come off as warm, generous, and attentive at the beginning of a relationship. They fool women into believing that they are the whole package. These people are master manipulators that have developed an art out of getting under the skin of women and inducing feelings that get women attached to them.

Even the most assured of women can fall for such a person because even though their intuition might blare warning sounds, this person figures out the things that make a woman feel most wanted, needed, and loved. Those are addictive feelings because at our core, everyone wants to find that person that feels like their other half.

Slowly but surely the narcissist reveals their true nature, though because no one can hold onto a façade forever even if they wanted to. However, by the time that the red flags are apparent, the narcissist has sunk his claws so deep into the woman that she cannot get free easily. Her emotions are entangled and the future that the narcissist has made her believe to be possible is in danger of ruination. This is why many women stay in such relationships even after the narcissist reveals his true nature.

Human beings are deeply social creatures and once we have formed an emotional attachment to another person, it is not easily dissolved and left in the past. We either become blind to this person's undesirable trait or excuse their behaviors. While logic may tell us to run in the other direction, our hearts can supersede these thoughts in an effort to maintain that connection. This makes moving on difficult, hence why the narcissist is able to reel us back in, even when we try to dissolve the relationship.

Prolonged exposure to a narcissist also diminishes mental and emotional health and tarnishes self-image. This person belittles other people. This can be a full-frontal attack or so covert that it is only realized after the damage is done. The victim's self-esteem and self-confidence suffer, while the narcissist has their ego stroked because the victim is likely seeking out their attention even after the maltreatment. The woman may feel that she is unworthy of true love and learns to accept this abuse.

Another reason it is so hard to let go of a narcissistic relationship is because it is hard to accept that we have been fooled so completely by another person. We yearn to believe that at least some of the things we based that relationship on is true, so we stay to search it out.

Also, many women harbor the false belief that they can change or help a narcissist. No one but the narcissist can take the steps necessary to change themselves. Getting the help, they need means seeking the counsel of a mental health provider or a trusted doctor so that they can gain the tools to build their self-esteem and self-confidence. This means that the narcissist has to confront his or her faults and inner demons, and work from the inside out to balance their emotions and solve their mental anguish.

This is a difficult task to do and is not an overnight process by any means. But only after this is done can a narcissist be able to have healthy interactions with other people. I say all of this to stress that women the world over need to recognize that they need to work on themselves so that they can be happy and leave these narcissistic men to deal with their own inner demons because there is no fixing someone who does not realize that they are flawed in such a fundamental way.

The reasons for entering such a relationship are irrelevant at the end of the day. What truly matters is moving on. To do that, you need to stop blaming yourself. Accept that you were deceived by a master manipulator and pathological liar. You are not the first and you will not be the last.

The true blame falls on the narcissist, but do not wait for this person to realize their faults and come to you with the closure you need. You need to claim that for yourself. You can start the process without an acknowledgment or apology from this person because that is part of your power as a strong woman. Now that you see past the lies and deceit, and understand the psychology of how this person hooked you, you can leave them in the past and move into the future where you are better able to spot similar people so that you defend your honor and worth.

Chapter 2

So many parts I identify with... frustrating first dating Brian

Marriage with a Narcissist

Romantic relationships with narcissists follow a predictable pattern if you know what to look for. There are 4 phases to a relationship with a narcissist. They go like this:

1. The honeymoon phase
2. The devaluation phase
3. The discard phase
4. The healing phase

The first three phases are led by the narcissist's desires and can repeat themselves over and over again unless a woman puts a stop to the cycle for good. Only after the woman has been able to move past the third phase is she able to embrace the fourth. This book is about helping you reach that fourth phase.

However, before you are able to do that, you need to understand what the first three phases look like so you can identify the pattern in your own relationship with a narcissist. This will allow you to finally get the closure that you need as well as enhance your ability to recognize if you are falling into another trap that involves a narcissist partner.

The Overvaluation Phase

The biggest feature of this phase in a relationship with a narcissist is being love bombed. That is why it goes by other names such as the honeymoon phase or the love phase. To the victim, it will indeed feel like a honeymoon – the place where great positive emotions and affection are in the spotlight and the place where it feels like nothing can go wrong. This is by design because that is exactly how the narcissist wants the woman to feel.

The narcissist's aim is to ensure that the victim is firmly attached to him by using grand professions of love, giving lots of compliments, and promising commitment to someone that is completely dedicated to her. This person is generous with his time, attention, effort, and affirmative words, all ingredients to make a woman feel like she is the most beautiful, the smartest, the most graceful, the best cook... He makes her feel that she is the best at everything.

This promotes the development of infatuation, which is often confused with love. But in fact, what the narcissist is doing is promoting obsession. This person is making it so that you cannot survive without their devotion. This person is making me so that you feel incomplete without their compliments and receiving their time and attention. This person is building an attachment.

This happens because this person is activating the reward center of the victim's brain. The reward center of the brain is the part that aids learning and development because when a person accomplishes something or is involved in activities that invoke positive emotions, the reward center floods the body with hormones that make the person feel good.

We all want to feel good, so we will continue to do the things that cause the flood of these hormones. This is why positive feedback is a technique that is involved in creating desired activity during childhood and in workplaces and schools. Hearing praise immediately activates the reward center of most people.

Every time the victim receives a compliment or is the recipient of this person's time and attention, hormones such as dopamine are released. This makes the victim feel happy and euphoric - in love.

Dopamine is the same hormone that is released when a cocaine or heroin addict gets a high. I am sure that you can see the correlation as to why it is so hard to keep away from a person who is love bombing you. Just like an addict going without a fix, going without this person's time, love, and attention will make you feel withdrawal symptoms when you stop receiving it. So, why would you put yourself through that pain of withdrawal when you can be showered with such dedication? The answer is that most people will not be able to find the willpower to

– especially if they have not been shown a good reason to. The involvement of hormones creates a dependency.

The narcissist makes his victim feel like she has found her soulmate because he will show her falsely that they have so many things in common. This person would have put in time and energy to know what pleases you and will give the illusion that they will provide all of these things. Is it any wonder that women who fall victim to narcissistic relationships when they think that they have found the one? The one who is in tune with their dreams, beliefs, and aspirations. The one that they can truly let their hair down with and drop their guard. The one who will be accepting of all of their flaws and still love them completely. The one who just gets them.

The narcissist is also benefiting from this phase because, of course, the victim will also dish out lots of love and attention by virtue of the simple fact that they are the recipient of it. Their self-esteem and self-worth get boosted by the accomplishment of hooking this person to them so thoroughly.

The narcissist loves being the center of attention and the center of other people's world. The reward center of their brain is also activated and as such, they will continue to love bomb the other person to gain the gratifying feelings that the release of hormones ensures. At this stage of a narcissistic relationship, even the narcissist feels infatuated. Of course, it would be easy for him to continue to shower the victim with praise and devotion.

But this phase of such a relationship is not sustainable because the narcissist is not being his true self. So, eventually, cracks will appear in his façade and then the devaluation phase begins. By then, his mission would have been accomplished though. He would have been able to make his victim addicted to him.

The Devaluation Phase

In the love bombing phase of a narcissistic relationship, the victim becomes completely open and trusting of the narcissist. Most likely, without even realizing it, this person places their emotional health and well-being in the narcissist's hands. There may have been vague warning signs in the overvaluation stage of a relationship with a narcissist, but because the victim was so starry-eyed and hooked on the narcissist, she will let them go unnoticed or brush them aside as insignificant compared to all the benefits she gets from being in a relationship with this person. Besides, no one is perfect, right?

But then these warning signs become too much to ignore and this sets the stage for this phase of a relationship with a narcissist. This stage is where the red flags start to show up.

This phase gets its name because the value the narcissist seemingly placed on the victim is taken away and this leaves the victim reeling. The narcissist will devalue the association with the victim by pulling away and taking away the things that they made so important to the victims such as their time, energy, and attention. The narcissist can do this seemingly overnight or gradually.

Where they were gladly attentive and gracious with compliments in the overvaluation stage, they will suddenly turn indifferent and ghost the victim. This can manifest itself in the narcissist not been available in times where the victim is in need or distress such as when she is combating an illness. The narcissist may even show no concern if the victim is in a potentially dangerous situation.

The narcissist can go weeks without allowing contact and because the narcissist has so thoroughly enchanted the victim at the beginning of the relationship, the victim will begin to wonder what she did wrong. This often leads to the victim feeling that they cannot survive without the narcissist despite the punishment that this person is putting them through.

This phenomenon is known as Stockholm syndrome. Named after a 1973 robbery in the town of Stockholm in which the robbers made hostages develop positive feelings towards them even though they were the target of a crime, this condition causes the development of sympathy and empathy to someone who has wronged us. It is not uncommon for persons in hostage and kidnapping situations to develop these feelings towards the captors. It is also not uncommon to hear that victims of abusive relationships harbor the same feelings towards their abuser.

For an empathetic person, it may be hard to see why the narcissist will do this if he was getting benefits such as the attention he craves in the overvaluation phase of the relationship. But the reason for this is simple. The narcissist encouraged this relationship for the thrill of the chase. He wanted to become the center of the person's world and when he has accomplished his goals, he will become bored. The narcissist was trying to fill a void within himself so that his self-esteem and self-worth would skyrocket. That was done and now the victim is no longer fulfilling their purpose.

At this stage, the narcissist is also experiencing devaluation even though the signs may not be obvious to other people. The self-worth and self-esteem of the narcissist are taking a nosedive once more and this leaves this person easily agitated. This makes them lash out and blame the victim. The narcissist also withdraws from the victim and this can often be done in a cruel way, especially if the victim tries to cling on to the relationship that used to be. In fact, the narcissist can gain benefit from this person clinging on to them by withdrawing further and tormenting this person with criticism and blame.

As the narcissist tears down the victim's self-esteem and confidence, this boosts their own self-esteem and self-confidence. Therefore, the narcissist will continue to do just enough to keep the victim invested in them and use this person as a punching bag for their own inadequacies. Unfortunately, the narcissist can make this a literal translation and become physically violent.

The narcissist will never own up to his derogatory behavior and will lie, cheat, and generally engage in self-serving behavior. Such a master manipulator, the narcissist will find a way to turn this around on the victim, laying the blame firmly at the victim's feet. This is why the devaluation stage of a narcissistic relationship is characterized by lots of anger, resentment, and fighting.

This would be the perfect time for the victim to leave this relationship but because that emotional attachment has been formed and because the reward center of the brain was activated in the love stage phase, this person will desperately try to regain the feelings that they had at the beginning of the relationship. This leads to the victim suffering from a lot of self-blame and self-loathing.

This negative mental state is most oven the result of verbal devaluation. This verbal devaluation is often triggered by the victim beginning to speak up for herself or confronting the narcissist about his behavior. The narcissist perceives this as a threat and is highly likely to retaliate with verbal devaluation techniques such as:

- Insults.
- Threats of abandonment.
- Withholding critical information, affection, or sexual intimacy.
- Demanding entitlement of information, affection, or sexual intimacy.
- False accusations.
- Gaslighting, which is a manipulation technique that covertly makes a person doubt their own sanity,

memory, perception, or judgment. This is a form of emotional abuse.

Gaslighting is something that the victims of narcissistic relationships need to be aware of because it is a subtle form of manipulation that has a huge impact. Signs that you are being gaslighted include:

- Often questioning whether or not your response to the narcissist is appropriate because this person makes you feel as if you are being unreasonable.
- Constantly excusing this person's behavior.
- Isolating yourself from friends and family.
- Finding it increasingly difficult to make decisions without consulting the narcissist.
- Feeling a little pleasure in the activities that you used to enjoy it before you started associating with the narcissist.
- Often feeling hopeless.
- Apologizing to the narcissist often.
- Often blaming yourself when things go wrong, even without prompting from the narcissist.
- Feeling like everything that you do is wrong.
- Have a general sense that something is wrong, but not being able to pinpoint what it is.

Being gas lighted can completely throw a person off their axis. Narcissists know how effective this form of manipulation is because it targets a person's vulnerabilities. The narcissist uses that information to make you doubt yourself on a fundamental level.

Just so that you can spot them in the future, here are a few examples of gaslight situations:

- Having your feelings trivialized such as the narcissist saying, "You always feel sorry for yourself for no good reason."
- The narcissist saying things that they will later deny even though you have a clear memory of the incident.
- The narcissist telling you that other people are talking about you behind your back.
- Having the narcissist hide physical objects from you then denying knowledge of it.
- The narcissist deliberately insisting that you were or were not at a location to deliberately confuse you.

I point out this manipulation technique to help you realize the extent to which a narcissist can delve into your psyche to control you. Being able to spot these tactics is a defense mechanism that is priceless.

The Discard Phase

Think of a narcissistic relationship as a situation where a greedy kid keeps taking candy out of a bag. This kid will keep dipping his fingers into the bag and consuming its contents, often at lightning speed, because it fulfills a selfish need within him. Eventually though, the bag will become empty and the kid will lose interest because he is no longer gaining fulfillment. The child will discard the bag and move on to the next best thing.

That about sums up the discard phase of a narcissistic relationship. You are the bag of candy and the narcissist is the kid. After the narcissist has taken everything he can from you, he will move on to someone else who can fulfill the needs within him. It is easy for the narcissist to move on because his feelings were never fully engaged in the first place. But the victim's feelings were engaged and this abandonment leads to hurt and confusion. Not only is that tough enough to deal with but, because the narcissist took all that he could from the victim, the victim is also left a shadow of the person that they used to be. Life will seem hopes and they will, even if for a short time, value their worth to be less than dirt.

This person will need to gather the inner strength needed to refill themselves with the goodness that they had before. This person will need to be proactively engaged in building their self-esteem and self-confidence to what it needs to be to honor their true worth.

Unfortunately, this is hardly ever a clean cut and dry process. The narcissist can drag the victim along for years, giving them just enough false hope to keep them available for the narcissist's benefit if he so chooses. The narcissist is only able to accomplish this because he has locked the victim in with lies and has often convinced this woman that no one else will love her or that she is unworthy of true love and dedication.

The Healing Phase

If the narcissist is stringing you along in the discard phase of the relationship, you need to gather your strength and walk away. Discard the hope that this person will change or that they will see fault in their actions. The best thing to do is block all contact with this person so that you cannot possibly be pulled back in by their lies again. The fact is that there is a real possibility that the narcissist will keep popping up in your life if you allow this because this person reserves the right to come back at any time to make use of the energy that you provide to recharge their sense of self-worth and self-esteem.

Only after you have blocked contact can you move on to this phase, which is healing and recovery.

The first part of this phase is accepting that you did nothing to deserve what that man put you through and that the fault lies with the narcissist. There is something fundamentally wrong with this person and no amount of support on your end will change that or help fix this person. Only that person is responsible for mending the damage within himself.

Move on and focus on you.

That needs to be your mantra during this phase. Free yourself from this man's control and manipulation once and for all and make yourself to your highest priority. This is how you will ensure that you never fall into a narcissist's trap again.

Why Did I Marry a Narcissist?

Healing will take you down a path where there is a lot of introspection and self-questioning. As you examine your past relationship with a narcissist, you will wonder how you ever fell for this man far less married him and believed that you two could have a happily ever after story. This question often arises because women focus strongly on the devaluation phase of the relationship because it is the start they reconcile to the trauma that they suffered.

Do not fall under the impression that the love phase of a relationship with a narcissist lasts for a few days or weeks. Remember that the narcissist only enters a relationship to get the things that he needs. Romantic relationships offer comfort, stability and emotional security. Sometimes they can even offer upgraded social status. As long as the narcissist is getting what he needs from love bombing his victim, he will continue to do so. Therefore, the narcissist can maintain the love phase for years.

After years of being in a relationship, the aim is usually toward marriage and the narcissist will offer that if it suits his purpose. That is why some women are left completely befuddled after the narcissist shows his true colors after years of marriage. There is no need for confusion. The circumstances unfolded in that manner because that is how it benefits the narcissist most.

Narcissists typically target empaths, that are highly emotionally intuitive and sensitive individuals. They become easily attuned to the emotions of other people. They can feel the pain of other people it seems at times. Empaths are the stark opposite of narcissists. Just like narcissism, this is a spectrum condition and people display varying degrees of this ability.

Naturally empathic people are good listeners and naturally giving. These people have the following qualities:

- Are able to absorb the emotions of other people. Because empaths are so highly intuitive, they feel the good and bad emotions that other people have. They can help shoulder the load of both negative and positive emotions of other people. Positive emotional absorption like peace can help them flourish while absorbing negative emotions like anger or anxiety depletes empaths.
- Placing the needs of others above the own. Because empaths have such huge hearts, they tend to give too much of themselves in an effort to relieve the pain of others. As such, many empaths lack the ability for effective self-care and overextend the special ability.
- Being easily overwhelmed in romantic relationships. Because of their propensity to absorb the emotions of the others as well as their natural inclination to put the needs of other people before their own, empaths can easily lose their identity in a romantic relationship if their partner does not produce that emotional stability in return.

Other common traits of empaths include being introverted with a need for a lot of alone time and being replenished by the natural world.

You may not realize it, but if you attracted a narcissist's attention, there is a high probability that you are a strong empath. If that is true, you can see the benefits the narcissist gained from marrying you. A strong empath can provide the emotional sustenance that a narcissist needs for years and so, the narcissist will maintain the façade for all that time.

A narcissist and an empath can never exist in a healthy relationship because one party is constantly giving while the other is constantly taking. This creates an imbalance and eventually, the person giving will have nothing left to give and the person taking will leave because there is nothing left to take.

Do not judge yourself harshly for being roped into marrying a narcissist. Always keep it in the back of your mind that this person is a master manipulator who has perfected the art of controlling events and people so that they gain their selfish needs.

Chapter 3

Divorcing a Narcissist

Divorce for anyone, whether or not they have been married to a narcissist, is very difficult. Considerations such as religion and belief system play a huge part, and some people really do believe that they should stick with another person through it all, through the good and the bad, through sickness and in health, till death do you part no matter what qualities this person displays, even physical violence.

I am not here to preach to you what your belief system should be or to tell you that you should discard your religious beliefs. Those are your personal preferences and decisions and I have no say in whether they are right or wrong.

What I am saying is that you should know your worth and you should never be subjected to the kind of manipulation and control that severe narcissistic personality disorder can inflict on the victim. Divorce should be a serious consideration if your narcissistic partner is displaying characteristics such as:

- Allowing emotions to dominate his thinking and having that be a reflection in his behavior.
- Taking everything personally.
- Avoidance of his responsibility in the problem.
- Constantly blaming others.
- Being unable to accept the loss or defeat.
- Being rigid and uncompromising.

No one should be expected to leave the rest of their life with such a negative influence on it. The kicker is that when you file for divorce from a narcissist, more than likely, this person will attempt to still enforce control over your life. This is doubly true if you have children with this person as you can never truly break the bond that you two have shared. In such a case, child visitation and co-parenting need to be a consideration in the separation.

The narcissist may use this condition to worm his way back into your life, especially if you show confusion, weakness, sympathy, or fear. The narcissus will feed off these emotions and continue to inflict his influence over you.

The only way to protect yourself from this is to be firm in your decision to divorce this person. No matter how you feel inside, this means showing no weakness to this person. You know that the narcissist is a liar, so do not buy into anything that he has to say. Also, be willing to enforce your legal rights to ensure that you, and your children if it applies, remain protected.

Why it is Difficult to Divorce a Narcissist

Getting to the point where you say enough is enough and take the steps necessary to sever the connection with a narcissist does not come easy. This becomes harder the longer a victim has been involved in the overvaluation phase of a relationship with a narcissist. There is a push and pull in a relationship with a narcissist that is all-consuming because despite how low the lows of this relationship, the highest will also high. Those highs are addictive.

The attachment that a victim feels to a narcissist despite knowing better is called a trauma bond. It is quite similar to Stockholm syndrome. A trauma bond is one that develops between a victim and an abuser. The abuser uses the victim's feelings of excitement, fear, emotional feelings and sexual psychology to entangle this person to them.

Victims of a narcissistic relationship developed codependency issues because they felt so loved and cared for in the beginning. Even as these feelings erode over time and with the revelation of the narcissist's true nature, the emotional mental attachment remains firm because while the victim might understand that the relationship structure has changed, she does not understand why it is occurring.

This lack of understanding makes her believe that if she just makes the effort to understand why the relationship is falling apart, then she could take the steps necessary to get back to the love bombing part of the relationship.

As a result, the victim finds it very difficult to enforce boundaries in the relationship. The weaker the victim's will of the enforcement becomes, the more complete the control the abuser has.

Also, the stronger a trauma bond is, the more likely the victim is to support the abuser's abusive behavior and the abuser's reasons for it. Because of this support, the victim with develop negative feelings towards any person who tries to assist her in moving on from such a dangerous situation.

How a Trauma Bond Develops

The development of the trauma bond is not magic. It is science. Surviving any sort of trauma activates a part of the brain known as the survival brain. It makes use of the part of the brain known as the amygdala. This part of the brain does not use reasoning skills or logic. It simply develops instinctive reactions to threats and as such, the goal is simple - survival. This instinct is so strong that it actually suppresses logical decision-making in an effort to ensure that the victim survives the drama. This part of the brain also releases hormones that enforce the bond such as oxytocin, endogenous opioids, corticotropin-releasing factor, and dopamine.

One of the simplest yet most effective survival techniques is forming bonds with other people. There is safety in numbers. Most often a narcissist will trap the victim into cutting ties with other people in their life. The narcissist becomes the only person in the victim's life, ensuring that there is no one else to form an attachment to. The trauma bond ensures that the victim remains trapped in an endless cycle because the victim will remain in that relationship as a mode of survival.

The victim is not thinking about the long-term implications of such a relationship because this part of the brain is only concerned with ensuring that the victim survives in the short run. For example, a woman who is being physically abused by a narcissist may feel that if she employs a long-term strategy like running away, then the narcissist may kill her compared to if she stays and endures, then she will survive. Because of this reasoning, the victims of narcissistic relationships develop a passive attitude towards being abused.

<u>If the victim of a trauma bond finally does find the strength to walk away, the narcissist is cunning enough to switch tactics and cycles back to the first phase of a narcissistic relationship</u>. <u>This reawakens the reward center of the brain and, therefore, strengthens the trauma bond that the victim has developed.</u>

Stages of a Narcissist Trauma Bond Formation

To develop a resistance of developing or maintaining a trauma bond with a narcissist, you need to be able to identify what it looks like. This makes it easier to break away from the connection because the sad part is that most victims are not aware that they have developed this destructive bond with a narcissist.

That is why there are so many instances and examples of women in relationships that are obviously abusive and toxic. The toxicity is not obvious to them only to other people who are looking in from the outside. The victim does not know that the narcissist that they cling to has never loved them and will never love them despite their efforts.

A trauma bond is developed in 7 steps. They are:
1. **Love bombing.** The narcissist comes on strong and gives lots of love, adoration, and validation to activate the reward center of the victim's brain. He will not ask for anything in return during this phase. This free giving secures the victim's feelings.
2. **Dependency develops.** Because of the consistency of the narcissist, the victim will become conditioned to expect the feelings that narcissist stirs within them. They start to feel secure in the relationship that is developing. During this phase, the narcissist is no longer giving love, attention, and validation for free. He will make the victim feel that she needs to do or give something to gain these rewards. This is likely covert and the victim does not even realize that it is happening.
3. **Withdrawal**. The narcissist begins to withhold the love, attention, and validation that he was given so easily to the victim and becomes unpredictable with how he will deliver such conditions. The blame and criticism start.

4. **Gaslighting commences.** The narcissist will make the victim feel as though everything that is going wrong in the relationship is her fault. The narcissist will encourage the victim to think that as long as she complies with the needs and desires of the narcissist, then things will return to how they used to be in stage 1. This is typically where the abuse in a narcissistic relationship begins, but because the victim has been conditioned to think that everything is her fault, she will not leave.
5. **Heightened control.** The narcissist strengthens his control over the victim and reinforces that things will only return to the love-bombing phase of the relationship if the victim does everything precisely as the narcissist says.
6. **Resignation**. The victim becomes resigned to the abusive situation. This is because the victim begins to lose her sense of self and as such, begins to lose a sense of the boundaries that she had before this relationship. This is because the narcissist has punched holes in the victim's self-esteem and has left his person confused and unhappy.
7. **Trauma bond established.** The victim is addicted to the narcissist's approval and is no longer thinking rationally. The trauma bond is complete at this stage and this is where the obvious is not so obvious to the victim because the narcissist has family planted himself into the mind of the victim.

Symptoms That a Person Suffers from a Narcissistic Trauma Bond

Not sure if you display signs of a trauma bond? The symptoms listed below will help you figure it out:

- Receiving just a few crumbs of affection, love, and validation from the narcissist makes your day. Receiving even a little bit of the validation and other positive emotions that the victim received in the first stage of the relationship puts them on cloud nine because the reward center is activated at the narcissist's will.
- Feeling stuck in the relationship and see no way out. Many times, it is not that the victim cannot physically leave. The intense longing to be close to the narcissist is what confines the woman to that relationship.
- Feeling that the narcissistic partner will be the only one who is able to fulfill your needs, even though this person is not currently doing so.
- Worrying that your actions and words will set the narcissists off. Walking on eggshells around the narcissist is common and a great sign of trauma bonding.
- Your brush off or excuse the narcissist's bad behavior, even when confronted by friends or family about it.
- You often feel that there is a level of "prey and predator" in the interaction of that relationship and that your vulnerabilities are being exploited

- You are aware that you are being deceived by the narcissist but still cannot say that the ties of the relationship.
- You feel shame at the things she had done, accepted and endured in this relationship.

Reading these symptoms can be disheartened because victims of narcissistic relationships suffered from some if not all of these symptoms. You likely recognized yourself and your behaviors within these signs.

Do not despair though. The trauma bond is hard to break, but it is not a possible task. The rest of this book is dedicated to helping you do just that.

Tactics for Dealing with and Severing a Narcissistic Trauma Bond

A trauma bond is likened to a drug addiction because it gives feelings of euphoria and then sucks them away. We know of instances where persons have beaten drug addiction, so women who suffer from a trauma bond developed from narcissistic relationships have the same hope.

The hope is only facilitated by taking action. There are a few tactics that you can employ to finally break free of that trauma bond that you have developed with your narcissistic husband. They include:

- Taking it one day at a time. It is easy to become overwhelmed when making decisions about your future and moving on from a narcissistic relationship. This can make it seem easier to just

stick with the status quo. You cannot allow that to happen. Therefore, to ensure that you move on for good, make one decision at a time and move on one day at a time.
- Committing to living in reality. The trauma bond is sustained by fantasies that things can be different and that a narcissistic partner can change. Remember that narcissism can only be dealt with by the narcissist. Therefore, you need to pull yourself out of the fantasies and deal with what is actually happening, and the reality is that this person is toxic to your health in all ways. The only reasonable response to that is getting rid of that toxicity.
- Living in the here and now. A lot of the fantasies that sustained a trauma are founded on what could be and what will be if you only just do what the narcissist outline. Stop that detrimental psychology by being aware of how you feel now and what is happening now. That is the only way that you will notice that this person is compromising your sense of self-worth and self-love. That will allow you to notice the obvious that can stop being obvious. Stop waiting for a change and act on what is happening now.
- Acknowledge your role in the narcissistic relationship. The narcissist would have placed all the blame on your shoulders for the things that went wrong. However, you need to take a step back and put things in perspective. If you really were as bad as this person said, then he would

have walked away. The point that he had not supported the fact that he was using you. Putting things in perspective gives you the opportunity to see the obvious and break free of the emotional prison.
- Allowing yourself to feel. There are a lot of messy emotions involved in being in a toxic relationship and sometimes, it can seem easier to just not feel them. However, the only way you can get past them is to feel them and acknowledge them for what they are. Then you can develop the techniques necessary to manage them in a healthy way.
- Allowing yourself to grieve. By severing your trauma bond with a narcissist, you allow this relationship to die. Grief is one of the necessary phases for getting over any death or loss.
- Committing to self-care. Self-care is not just a physical endeavor. It is about emotionally and mentally caring for yourself as well. A narcissist will teach his victim to discard such personal caring. Therefore, to counter this, start making decisions that focus on your needs and wants. It is time to think about what is best for you and the first step to doing that is being compassionate and understanding towards yourself. Stop beating yourself up about the decisions that you made in the past and start encouraging yourself to do better towards uplifting and empowering yourself.
- Making a list of personal boundaries that must be honored by the other party if you were to ever be

in a romantic relationship again. These boundaries are meant for both you and the other party. Boundaries can be simple such as not entertaining a man who drinks heavily or not allowing someone else to take control of your finances no matter what. The point is that writing this will solidify them in your mind and, therefore, allow you to recognize when these boundaries are being trespassed by another person.

- Developing a healthy support system. The narcissist may have achieved his goal of cutting the links that you had with other people, but this is the time in your life where you must commit to rebuilding old connections or developing new ones that are not centered on drama and negative emotions. Healing from a trauma bond all the more difficult if you have no one around you to show you care and concern. If you do not have that ready support in your life, do not be afraid to reach out to a trained medical health professional.
- Allowing yourself to think of your life as bright and fulfilling without this person. Envision what it would be like to have a partner that is supportive and uplifting rather than one that displays behaviors that encourages the development of a trauma bond. Envision your life doing things as an individual so that even if your future does not have a romantic relationship, you will still be happy and fulfilled. Hold onto that vision and start implementing measures that will allow you to make it a reality. Such measures can include starting new

hobbies, joining clubs, and furthering your education.

The Best Practices for Getting through a Divorce from a Narcissist as Unscathed as Possible

We have established that divorce is a difficult thing to go through, but divorcing a narcissist has its own set of unique challenges. Most than likely the process will become drawn out in court, especially if the woman initiated the process. The narcissist will feel the need to punish her for this. Drawing out the process is also a way to maintain contact and attempt to manipulate in addition to still receiving attention. The narcissist does not give up anything willingly and is not good at accepting defeat.

The first thing you need to do is not let the narcissist know that you are leaving. Plan ahead and just do it because the only way that you can maintain control of the situation is to distance yourself from the emotional abuse, gas lighting, and control that the narcissist tries to enforces.

You already know what you have certain weaknesses to this person. This person knows this as well. That is why their manipulation has worked so well in the past. Stop letting them use those weaknesses against you. If you tell a narcissist that you intend to leave them, they will just revert to acting out stage 1 of the narcissistic relationship whereby slightly trapping you by activating the reward system of your brain. Do not allow that to happen in the first place by simply removing yourself from the situation.

This is especially important if there is physical abuse involved in that relationship. In that case, the narcissist may lose control and inflict pain upon the victim.

Other practices you can employ to make the divorce from a narcissist as painless for you as possible include:

- Try to assert your financial independence from the narcissist before for you to leave. Again, this is something that you need to keep to yourself. Steadily and secretly stock up on funds as much as possible so that this person cannot manipulate you in a financial sense. This is especially true if there are children involved. In that case, you need to be able to support both yourself and your children.
- Keep copies of everything, especially financial expenditures. Gather as much evidence as you can to support your case during the divorce the better.
- Ensure that the narcissist cannot track your actions after you have left. Do this by logging out of all your online accounts such as social media and online banking. Changing your password is also an added security measure. It is also pertinent to find out if the narcissist has other means of tracking you such as using the location feature on your mobile devices. Signs that your mobile devices are being tracked include inconsistent login information if your device has the Kindle reading app installed and a battery that runs low

frequently. You can use a remote access tracker to find out if the narcissist is tracking your location and to disable it.
- Cut off communication with other toxic people in your life, especially those that support the actions of the narcissist. Divorcing a narcissist is not only an opportunity to get rid of his toxic influence, but to also get rid of the other toxic influences in your life.
- Report the abuse that you have suffered at the hands of the narcissist. This is especially necessary in cases of physical abuse, but it does not mean that you have to go to the police. Just let anyone know such as your doctor or a trusted friend so that there is a record that can protect you in the future if push comes to shove.
- Ensure that you have competent and reliable legal counsel during the divorce. This person needs to be proactive in getting you the things that you deserve out of divorce.
- Do not negotiate or settle during the divorce proceedings unless it benefits you to do so. The narcissist knows that drawing out the divorce process can make you easier to manipulate and pressure. Do not buy into this pressure and allow your legal counsel to advise you on how to get what you deserve out of the process.

The Benefits of Divorcing a Narcissistic Husband

Being single is difficult after you have been in a romantic relationship even if that relationship was nothing to be desired. We as human beings have a need for connection with other people and that need is more so apparent by the formation of romantic pairings. This is because of the psychological needs that we have. These needs include:

- Needing to feel loved. This need for love starts from the moment we are born. A baby needs to receive love from its parents to develop in a healthy way. A child who does not receive this basic need typically has social, emotional, mental, and behavioral problems growing up and this extends to their adulthood.

- Needing to feel important. We all want to feel that our existence matters to at least one other person. This need manifests itself in doing meaningful tasks, contributing to the community, acquiring wealth, and starting a family. The last item needs a partner to accomplish. Also, simply having someone to come home to and knowing that someone misses their presence is basic, but has a huge impact on making a person feel wanted.
- Needing security. We want to feel safe and comfortable in our environment. Knowing that we can obtain health care if sick, having a home to shelter up and knowing that someone is in our corner allows us to rest easy.

- Needing to contribute. Beyond our own need to grow and develop, we want to be part of someone else developments. It is human nature to leave a mark on the world in some way and helping the person with whom we have a romantic engagement will do that.

We enter romantic relationships to have these needs and others met. While, of course, no two persons or any relationship is perfect, a healthy relationship is one where both parties are having the majority of their met consistently by entering and remaining in the union. The victim of a narcissists marriage does not have these needs met on a consistent basis and if they are being met, there is some trade-off that is not healthy.

At the end of the day, you did enter into this union and now that you have realized that you are better off without it. Here are a few reasons to reinforce your decision and to make you realize that you will be all the better off without having this narcissistic personality in your life.

- Having this time to yourself will give you a chance to focus on you without the demands of anyone else intruding. You will no longer have to walk on eggshells and can freely be who you are.
- You will learn to rely on yourself more so that you do not feel the need to be in a relationship to be happy or fulfilled. This will show you that any relationship you contemplate entering is simply a complement to the life you have built for yourself rather than the focus of all your attention.

- You will realize just how strong you are because you would have come out of this relationship a survivor. Being able to survive a relationship with a narcissist and also set in motion a brighter future for yourself will make you realize that you can indeed to anything that you set your mind to.
- You will be able to control your own life and destiny without the input of someone who does not have your best interest at heart.
- You will learn to set healthy boundaries so that you will not tolerate unacceptable behavior from anyone else in your future.
- You will realize that there is a lot more to be gained from being your authentic self rather than closeting your true identity away to please someone.
- You will learn to appreciate life and success on your own terms.
- You will begin to learn more about yourself as you and fully embrace the fact that you have the freedom to do as you please, think as you please, and be free to be the person that you are.
- You will love yourself better and as such will demand better love from anyone else that you let into your life. This will give you the power to walk away if that unconditional love is not given a lot quicker and easier the next time around.
- You will gain a better perspective on what you want out of the marriage so that if you contemplate the union another time around, you will not be

persuaded by someone who will provide you with less than you deserve.

Chapter 4

Super Techniques and Power-ups for Recovery after a Narcissistic Marriage

Contained within this chapter are 4 powerful umbrella techniques that help pave the way to recovery after being in a marriage with a narcissistic husband. Each technique contains several power-up steps and each will be discussed.

Technique 1 – Seize Contact with the Narcissist

They say that absence makes the heart grow fonder, but in this case, the aim is to make the heart become detached. Breaking up after a long-term relationship is always a messy and complicated affair, but this is even more so the case when a woman is recovering from a narcissist relationship.

Confusion, loneliness, and pain are a terrible burden and naturally, we want to avoid it. The simplest way that comes to mind is often just staying in that relationship to not feel these things. The trauma bond magnifies those feelings, but the distance is the only way that you can break the hold that they have on your heart and the psychology of your mind.

It may be hard to do, but having no contact with your narcissist abuser is necessary for the following reasons:

- **It allows you to detox.** After being in a relationship with a narcissist, you are a mess of emotions and thoughts that typically do not belong to you. Just like when the body has accumulated toxins from eating in an unhealthy manner and needs a detox, the same applies to the mind and heart. You need to purge yourself of these feelings and thoughts, and mourn the loss of all you have giving to and giving up for this person so that you can allow yourself to just be - clean, healthy, and just you. Just like with a physical detox. This is a process that happens over time and that can only be facilitated by avoiding contact with this person. You are not going to eat fried chicken if you are detoxing, right?
- **It allows you to gain perspective.** Your feelings are largely involved in any type of romantic relationship and these feelings have been manipulated by a narcissist. The close distance to this person does not allow you to see clearly. However, distance can allow you to see all the things that are wrong with your relationship and the real reasons why it would have never worked out healthy.

- **It allows you to finally get over this person.** Just like mourning the death of someone, you need to go through several stages of grief before you can get over a relationship with a narcissist. If he is in your thought bubble often, you will never be able to go through the steps in the required order that will allow you to heal with time. You will never be able to see that you are happier, healthier, and more fulfilled without his presence. To blow out the flame that existed between you two are one point, you need to steer clear of this person.
- **It allows you to re-discover yourself.** The narcissist chipped away at everything that you were to replace that with an insecure and codependent person. In order to break this person's hold on you, you need to realize that you can stand on your own two feet soundly and be secure in your independence. That surety allows you to re-discover yourself and build the person that you want to be in the future.
- **It allows you to entertain the idea that you can have a better romantic relationship with someone who is concerned about your well-being, empowerment, and growth.** The narcissist worked hard to ensure that you did not see past them to see what is greater. I know it might be hard to believe but there are men out there who would be good to you and treat you in the way that you deserve. You will never find that man or be able to enjoy a fulfilling relationship if you are stuck in an abusive cycle with a narcissist.

The idea of no contact with this person can seem obscure but in essence, it means:

- No contact via phone calls, text messages, or emails.
- No answering of his calls, text messages or emails. My recommendation is that you block and delete his number.
- No interaction whatsoever on social media. This means no Facebook messages or commenting, no Snapchat, no tweets, no viewing of his Facebook status, etc. Also, it means no stalking his social media accounts. While this might not technically mean "contact," this action keeps you attached to him and is self-sabotaging.
- Do not go to places where you are likely to meet or see him.
- Do not go to the same places that you two used to frequent together.
- Do not check in with his friends or family about him.
- Do not look through old photos of the two of you together.

It might also be hard to define how long you should go without having contact with a narcissist, but it must be enough so that his presence and behaviors do not affect or move you. As a rule of thumb, I would give it at least 90 days of no contact – longer if you can manage it.

No contact can be difficult to achieve if you have children with this person. However, you can limit your interactions to discussions only about the children that you two have made together. If this person tries to steer the conversation in another direction, simply walk away or hang up the phone if the discussion is being made via that medium. Do not give this person a chance to have a conversation with you about anything else. Do not allow yourself to be fooled by his charm once more. Always remember that it is a facade that hides the real person underneath. If it is possible, have a third-party handle arrangement and discussions between you two about the children so that you can keep it 100% no contact.

Technique 2 – Reclaim Responsibility for Your Life

The narcissist may have taken control of your life temporarily, but as the strong woman that you are, I know that you will be able to get back on your feet in no time, especially since I will be showing you a few strategies that you can employ to reclaim responsibility for your hours and days.

The three techniques that I will share in this section include:

- Managing your personal energy
- Developing your intuition
- Setting effective goals

Manage Your Personal Energy

Reclaiming your power after someone has taken it away is a monumental task and you may be tempted to do everything all at once. However, that will only lead to being overextended. The reality is that you will not be able to do everything at once and therefore, you need to manage how you commit to getting things done so that you do not feel wiped out. This involves managing your personal energy.

What is Personal Energy?

This is also called willpower and entails how much vitality a person can maintain while performing daily tasks as well as this person's resolve when it comes to fulfilling goals and priorities. Personal energy is something that ebbs and flows like a wave. Sometimes, it is up and sometimes, it is down. The goal is to make it so that your personal energy has more up periods than down periods. It is only by managing your choices, thoughts, and emotions that you can promote an upward trend.

Being in a narcissistic relationship made your personal energy favor a downward spiral. Having your thoughts and emotions constantly taken up by that person was draining to you. Therefore, I am sure that you dealt with several periods of feeling chronically fatigued, hopeless and joyless.

Now that you are no longer within this person's reach, this is the time for you to learn to manage your personal energy so that you feel invigorated to take the steps necessary for pushing your life in the direction that you would like it to go.

The first thing you need to do when managing your personal energy is to handle your emotions. Your emotions are impacted by the things around you such as your friends, job, living space, and more. If these things make you feel stressed out and do not bring you joy, then you need to re-evaluate how much of an impact they should have on your life. You need to have things that inspire you, motivate you, and uplift you in your environment. Anything else needs to go.

Other things you can do to help invigorate you and boost your personal energy include:

- Listening to music that uplifts you.
- Partaking in more activities that make you feel happy.
- Spend more time in nature.
- Declutter your life. This is not just about ensuring that your space is neat and tidy. You also need to ensure that you are in good physical health, that your professional life helps develop your whole person, that your living arrangements suit you, that your finances are not a burden, that your interpersonal relationships have good communication, and that your mind and heart are at peace. Remove any clutter in any aspect that

does not help you achieve good emotional balance and, therefore, balanced personal energy. Anything that does not meet the criteria needs to be worked on.
- Learn to manage your time. This is about developing systems that allows you to plan your days and control how you spend your hours on specific tasks. This control not only allows you to be more efficient and productive with your days but also gives you a sense of accountability and a sense of purpose that does wonders for developing and maintaining your personal energy.

Develop Your Intuition

After being in an abusive relationship, opening up yourself again, even to yourself, can be a daunting task. Everyone wants the comfort, security, and love that comes with a romantic relationship, but you know first-hand how those needs and wants can be manipulated and used against you. You probably do not trust your own instincts anymore because you placed your heart on the line for someone who did not deserve it and you may be wondering why you did not see the danger from afar.

Constantly questioning yourself, erodes your self-esteem, self-worth, and self-confidence. Persons who have suffered abuse at the hands of a narcissistic partner continue to do this even after the relationship has been severed. This self-doubt also makes it difficult to move on with your life even if you have no contact with the narcissist. There is hope though to not only regain that instinctive trust in yourself but also to reclaim responsibility for your life and your decision-making. To do that, you need to stop second-guessing yourself. The only way to accomplish that is to get in touch with your intuition once more.

What Is Intuition?

If you have ever experienced a feeling that just tells you that you should act in a certain way or you have done something based on a hunch, then you know what intuition feels like. It goes by many names such as having a feeling in your bones, a funny feeling, a sixth sense, or gut feeling but it all comes down to the same thing. Your intuition is your ability to understand something instantly without clear, conscious reasoning.

Whether or not there is data at hand to be calculated, intuition helps us make decisions in rapidly changing environments. Intuition helps develop our leadership skills and keeps are safe in dangerous situations. However, sometimes we can lose touch with our intuition and oftentimes, it is because we lack trust within ourselves.

The power of female intuition is legendary. And while yours may have taken a hit, there is no better time to rebuild that instinctive gut feeling that will help guide you redevelop yourself and build the life that you want and deserve. The voice inside you that guides you may have gone quiet due to do narcissist's manipulations, but now that you are free of him, you can get in touch with that voice once more.

Powerful Ways in Which You Can Develop and Strengthen Your Intuition

- **Meditate**. There is a common misperception that meditation is about changing your personality, becoming a different person, or becoming a better person. Meditation is none of those things. Instead, it is about gaining an awareness of one's self and how your mind works. It quiets the unnecessary thoughts and noise that our environments can bash us with. This quietly can allow you to rekindle that spark with your intuition, especially if it has been quiet for a long time.
- **Engage in creative activities**. Such activities can include gardening, scrapbooking, and drawing. Getting your creative juices running also urges your inner voice to speak up.
- **Pay attention to your dreams**. When we are awake, the brain takes on many tasks in order to ensure our survival as well as all the activities that come with living. Even though the brain is just as active while you are asleep, the subconscious mind is often the power by intuition and, therefore, does not have the restrictions that would have normally been placed if you were in a wakeful state. Allow those subconscious happenings to help reawaken your intuition during your hours of wakefulness.

- **Pay attention to watch your five senses have to tell you.** Learn to stop and smell the roses. When you taste something, allow it to sit on your tongue so that you can see it. When you look at something, really look and when you hear something, pay attention to the decibels. Touch things so that you can truly feel the textures. Your five senses are powerful things that communicate a lot to you about your world. By using these five senses to the maximum potential, you gain access to your sixth sense, which is your intuition.
- **Take a step back from sometimes.** While it is a great idea to establish a daily routine to keep you on track, especially while you are in the process of rebuilding your life, it is also a good idea to surround yourself with new things and to slow down when necessary. Going on a retreat or a sabbatical where you are surrounded by a quiet and not overly sensitized to the fast-paced of urbanism allows your intuition to speak up.
- **Take action**. Second-guessing yourself continuously only stifles that inner voice. Allow your intuition to work its magic by taking action immediately so that you can lean on that inner wisdom more often.

The more you rely on your intuition, the greater it develops. As this voice gets stronger, you will be able to make decisions faster, create plans that help you with your future more efficiently, and solve problems quicker, so that you can achieve your goals for the future in a coordinated manner.

Set Goals for Yourself

Goal setting is a skill that anyone who wants a chance at developing a future they design needs to learn. Setting your goals allows you to walk a guided path that is more secure and not filled with the uncertainty of not knowing what your next move will be. Effective goal setting does not only pertain to one part in your life like your career. You need to grow as an entirety rather than only in one aspect. Therefore, these are the areas that you need to focus on while setting goals for your future:

- Personal development, which entails the physical, mental, emotional, and spiritual aspects of growing yourself as a whole person.
- Career, which involves your job and what else you do to earn an income.
- Physical health, which encompasses physical activities, eating habits, exercise routines, and other lifestyle choices that affect how you feel physically.
- Self-care, which is about the preservation of your emotional, mental, spiritual, and physical health.
- Home life, which is about the space and atmosphere that you live in.
- Extracurricular activities, which include vacation, hobbies, and other things that you would like to do with your free time.

- Relationships, which encompasses not only romantic dealings but also family, professional, and friendly interpersonal interactions.

Do not overwhelm yourself when you begin in your goal setting adventure. In every aspect of your life, list three things that are most important for you to develop. Of those three items, make one a priority and pursue it. Once you have accomplished that one item then you can move on to the next on the list.

Technique 3 – Release the Trauma You Suffered Back into the Universe

Handling emotional pain is not easy and instead of facing it, which many of us do not know how to do in the first place, we bury it and leave it untreated. Just like a physical wound, burying it under a bunch of bandages without treating it with the proper antiseptic, will only lead to infection and a greater injury than when you started.

Signs of emotional suppression include:

- Being uncomfortable when asked about how you feel about anything or anyone.
- Rarely crying or getting angry.
- Feeling uncomfortable around people who are highly emotional.
- Feeling like you need to be in control of everything all the time.

- A propensity to relying heavily on escapist behaviors such as oversleeping, binge-watching television, and video gaming.
- Feeling like you are overreacting if you get sad or angry.
- Thoughts that are most frequently negative or critical of yourself and other people.
- Often feeling low energy or tired for no apparent reason.
- Suffering from sleep problems.
- Being often forgetful or absent-minded.
- Suffering from ongoing stress or low-level anxiety.

Until you handle your emotions and release them in a healthy way, understanding and expressing your emotions will be problematic in your life. The kicker is that most people who are emotionally suppressed have no idea because not only do they try to hide their emotions, but they also try to avoid them and run away as much as possible instead of handling them properly. The hope is that this behavior will make the emotion disappear but it does not work that way. Rather, you only magnify the problem.

Remember that many persons who experienced narcissistic abuse in a relationship cope by taking on a passive attitude. This can only be done if emotions are buried. Otherwise, the victim would blow on the narcissist, cry, vent, and in general, not tolerate this treatment. But this person conditioned you to bury your emotions deep because they wanted their own to be in the spotlight at all times. After being trained to do this, you need to be active about taking a different approach to dealing with your emotions.

Doing this will likely be uncomfortable at first. But the key is to remember that you are human. No one is perfect and no one should be expected to always have perfect control of their emotions. You are a flawed person just like everyone else on this planet. As such, your emotions and how you express them will not be a perfect process each and every time. If you feel lousy one day, you should be allowed to express that just as you should be allowed to express when you feel angry, sad or moody. Negative emotions are part and parcel of being a human being. Expressing these negative emotions allow you to get rid of them so that you can enjoy the positive feelings when they come.

Expressing emotion comes with vulnerability and I am sure that you are trying to avoid such a situation since the narcissist taught you such a tough lesson in letting go and letting your guard down. But we all need someone that we can be our true selves with. All you need to do is teach yourself how to detach from people who are not deserving of that side of you, especially if they have already proven that they cannot or will not provide the support that you need and want.

How to Handle Suppressed Emotions

The first step in allowing your emotions to surface in a healthy and helpful manner includes being aware that they exist in the first place. You have to recognize that there is a problem in expressing yourself and what you feel. A good way to develop this awareness is by looking at yourself in the mirror. Admit to yourself that you have buried parts of yourself, including what you feel. Admit to yourself that this is unhealthy. Then make the resolve to do something about this. Say all of this out loud.

Once you have developed that awareness, the action that needs to take place is the dedication of time to just yourself. You cannot allow yourself to be vulnerable with other people if you do not first allow yourself to be vulnerable with yourself. The key to having effective 'you' time is to shut down everything and temporarily step away from everyone so that your feelings are your focus. This will allow you to listen to your intuition as well and this is the best voice for allowing you to speak to your emotions.

During this time, ask yourself questions. No question is too far-fetched or invalid. *What am I afraid of? What makes me sad? What makes me happy? If my craziest and most far-fetched dream were to come true, what would it be? What made me angry within the last week?* Do not rush your intuition to answer these questions. Instead, allow the quiet and solitude to marinate your thoughts, desires, and emotions. Delve deep into your mind and think these questions thoroughly, taking as long as you need for the answer to become apparent.

The next thing you need to do is cry. You went through terrible trauma and I'm sure you have been putting on a brave face in front of other people. Maybe you never even cry. I have counseled many women who believe that if they cry, they will break apart and there will be no way for them to put the pieces back together. They believe that they should be tough all the time because that will ensure that they do not get taken advantage of again.

However, not crying is not a sign of courage or bravery. It is actually the opposite. It means that you are not brave enough to face your toughest opponent, which is yourself and your emotions. You are running away – a cowardly act.

Since I know what a strong and courageous be in that you are, I encourage you to do one of the hardest things you might ever have to do. I encourage you to cry. You might have forgotten how but one of the most effective ways of encouraging these emotions to come to the surface is to think of a sad moment. Allow that memory to immerse your mind. Allow yourself to feel what you felt then. You can aid this process by listening to music or watching a movie that specifically relates to that time in your life when you felt what you felt.

Do not fight the emotions that surface. It will be painful. Expect that. Let the tears flow and sob. Scream if you must. It does not matter how long it takes or how puffy your eyes get, cry that ugly cry that you have been bottling up for too long. You are not being a crybaby. You are not being weak. Think of yourself as a warrior who is shedding an old skin so that she can upgrade to new better and stronger armor.

After you have cried, then it is time to learn to laugh. Suppressing emotion does not just bury your negative emotions. It also buries your positive emotions and takes away your ability to laugh freely and without censor. By trying not to be sad or mad, you forget how to be glad as well.

To bring that happy voice back, do things that make you laugh like watching comedies or reading funny tales. Laughing and smiling are exercises that release hormones that make you feel good. The good news is that faking it at the beginning helps release those same hormones because the brain sometimes cannot tell the difference between what is fake and what is real in that department. So look at yourself in the mirror and smile. Remember what it feels like to use these muscles. When you do laugh and smile for real, allow the feeling to flow through you so that you get reacquainted with it.

As you get reacquainted with the good, the bad and the ugly of your emotions, keep steadfast in your quest to set them free. Do not regress by ignoring them once more. Accept them for what they are and accept that they are part of you. When you feel emotional and need to cry, let it out. When you feel angry, learn to express that in an effective and efficient way. When you feel happy, there is nothing wrong with smiling or laughing.

Another tip is to not compare how you feel to have other people feel. There is no such thing as appropriate emotions at appropriate times. You feel what you feel when you feel it and that is it. That is what being yourself is about. Do not accept the judgement of other people in the wake of you expressing what you feel in a respectful manner and most importantly, do not judge yourself. As a person who has survived narcissistic abuse, you should be proud of yourself and proud of your strength for getting so far and allowing yourself to feel.

The next thing to do is learn to pamper yourself. The narcissist made sure that everything was about him. It is time to make it all about you and what you feel. This is not selfishness. This is self-preservation. This does not have to be extravagant or expensive. Something as simple as taking a few hours in the evening to take a warm bath, listen to some soothing music and surround yourself with a calming atmosphere can take you a long way. Make yourself feel special and cared for so that the next time you choose to let someone in, you know what behavior you should be expected from them because your body and mind have been reacquainted with what it feels like to be cared for in the right way.

Lastly, you need to learn to feel grateful for having these feelings to feel. You need to be grateful for your ability to manage them and being strong enough to confront them on a daily basis and not let them overwhelm you. You need to be grateful that you are emotionally free of the narcissist. No matter how painful the experience that you went through at the hands of the narcissist, that time was a learning experience that has brought you closer to being the person that you will greatly be in the future.

No matter what, remember to be grateful for that. One way to do that is to practice journaling. Every day, write something you are grateful for.

Tips for managing your emotions in the right way include:

- Focusing on the positives in your life, no matter how trivial they may seem.
- Learning to recognize when you talk negatively to yourself and replacing that with positive self-talk.
- Surround yourself with positive people who encourage you to not only be better, but laugh and experienced good things.
- Learn to stay present in the moment so that you experience the emotions of the time rather than being focused on the past or the future.

Technique 4 – Ensure That another Narcissist Does Not Take Advantage of You

One of the terrible injustices that the narcissist perpetrated against you was continuously trespassing your personal boundaries. This person did this to take away your sense of assertiveness and pressure you into being what he wanted you to be. You are now reclaiming your power and your life. This is the time that you need to draw a clear line in the sand so that anyone else who enters your life knows that these are the boundaries that you are set up and that there will be consequences if they were to overstep these lines.

What Are Personal Boundaries and Why Are They Important

Personal boundaries of physical, emotional, spiritual, and mental walls that every person creates to protect themselves from being violated, used, and manipulated by other people. These walls are built up with bricks made of personal morals and values and help a person distinguish who they are as a person and what they need and want from other people. The maintenance of strong personal boundaries is necessary for cultivating well-being and health in all aspects of your life.

Personal boundaries come in several types and they include:

- Intellectual boundaries, which allows you to feel entitled to your own thoughts and opinions in relation to other people.
- Spiritual boundaries, which allows you to feel entitled to your own spiritual beliefs in comparison to other people.
- Social boundaries, which allow you to feel entitled to pursue your own social activities and friends in relation to other people.
- Physical boundaries, which allow you to feel entitled to your own space, however wide that you need this to be in relation to other people.
- Time boundaries, which allows you to feel entitled to protect your time as a valuable asset to you.

- Sexual boundaries, which allows you to feel entitled to consent, respect, understanding, preference, and desires as it relates to sexual intimacy.
- Material boundaries, which allows you to feel entitled to entitle protect, give me borrow your material assets such as jewelry, home, car, and money as you please rather than at the expectation of someone else.

Having personal boundaries is a communication technique that conveys your sense of self-worth and self-respect to other people. Therefore, having no personal boundaries or weak personal boundaries leads to confusing your wants and needs with him the wants and needs of other people. That creates core dependency, which is excessive psychological or emotional reliance on anyone else. This was a situation encouraged and enforced by the narcissist. It will never be a healthy situation to have codependency in a relationship.

Having weak personal boundaries also makes a person feel as if they are not good enough, weak, or worthless. Having such low self-esteem creates self-doubt and negative feelings toward one's own character.

Are you unsure if you suffer from weak personal boundaries? You can help decipher that question by paying attention to the signs and symptoms such as:

- Saying yes to the requests, wants, and needs of other people even though you want to say no.

- Constantly feeling as if you are being taken advantage of by other people.
- Not speaking up when you are being mistreated.
- Verbally agreeing with other people even when you disagree.
- Allowing another person's touch even when you feel uncomfortable with the sensation.
- Feeling guilty for taking time for self-care.
- Feeling out of touch with your own needs.
- Being passive aggressive.
- Applying manipulative techniques to try to regain your lost power.
- Feeling guilty when other people are not happy because you have taken on their happiness as your responsibility.
- Feeling like you need to earn someone's respect by being nice.
- Being chronically fearful about what other people think of you.

If you suffer from at least 50% of the symptoms on that list, then you need to seriously consider doing what needs to be done to rebuild and reinforce your boundaries. Do not blame yourself if you have poorly constructed boundaries. Not only is this something that is not commonly taught to young children, but the narcissist that you were in a relationship with would have done everything he could have to destroy yours. Now that you are aware that they are weak. The responsibility is on you to build them into a steel-like structure.

Before I get to the techniques that can employ to develop strong personal boundaries, let's take a moment to discuss what personal boundaries are **not** so that you do not get confused in the future. Firstly, it is not selfish to have personal boundaries. You are striving to be an emotionally and mentally healthy person and believe me when I say that anyone with a good sense of self-respect and self-esteem has strong personal boundaries.

Secondly, many people believe that having good personal boundaries will cause people to dislike them and will make their relationships suffer. While this may be true, you will be all the better for it because these people do not have your best interests at heart. If they feel like that, you should compromise your personal boundaries for their own personal gain or pleasure. Therefore, not only will developing and enforcing personal boundaries help you truly understand the dynamics of your former relationship with a narcissist, but it will also help you recognize other relationships in your life that are toxic for you. Do not be disheartened by the fact that you may lose some relationships because you establish strong personal boundaries. The good news is that you are more likely to attract persons that are willing to be respectful of your needs and your boundaries. You will gain more authentic friends and personal relationships because of this establishment.

Next, there is a misconception that having personal boundaries will make you feel terrible about yourself. While you might feel comfortable standing up for yourself at first, you will realize that having personal boundaries and enforcing them makes you feel empowered and much happier because you are living your life on your terms rather than anyone else's.

Lastly, the myth I want to talk concerning personal boundaries is that they are rigid and uncompromising. This myth is untrue. Your boundaries are as flexible as you want them to be. That is not to say that you should compromise them at the slightest push-back from anyone but you can bend them to suit certain relationships. You need to be careful with this flexibility to ensure that this person is deserving of your compromise before that you do this. Also, boundaries are things that evolved over time. What may be a personal boundary for you today, may not be a personal boundary for you tomorrow and vice versa. You can even discover new personal boundaries from simple interactions with other people.

Once you have gotten past the myths and misperceptions, you can focus on the benefits of building strong personal boundaries. These benefits include:

- Speaking up for yourself more.
- Being able to comfortably say no when you do not want to do something.
- Being able to comfortably disagree with someone else.
- Having increased personal energy reserves.
- Feeling more emotionally balanced and therefore, happier.

- Spend more time caring for yourself and your needs without guilt.
- Having an increased sense of self-worth and self-esteem.
- Feeling free to be yourself and therefore, having more courage to express yourself.
- Feeling like you are more in control of your life.
- Attracting a more supportive and healthy friendship circle as well as romantic relationships.
- Feeling more appreciated and valued by the company that you keep and yourself.

How to Create Personal Boundaries That Do Not Get Trespassed by Other People

To effectively establish your boundaries, you need a pen and paper or a digital document for the exercise to follow. On a fresh page, create a title called *Your Limits*. Underneath this, list intellectual, spiritual, social, physical and the rest of the types of personal boundaries with adequate space kept between each type of personal boundary.

Next comes introspection. Examine past experiences that you had with work colleagues, friends, family members, strangers, and romantic partners. List all memories that you can re-discover where you felt angered, resentful, or discomforted due to interactions or encounters with these individuals. Categorize them based on the type of personal boundary that was crossed.

Creating this list allows you to specifically pinpoint instances where your boundaries were trespassed so that you are more easily identify if this happens again in the future. Continually come back to this list when you experience new instances where you feel like your boundaries have been overstepped. This list will also allow you to see what your needs are out of a relationship as well as what your current sense of self-esteem and self-worth are.

Next, list your values for each personal boundary type on a fresh page or document. This may take some time and will be a continuous process where you update your boundaries list as you discover them.

Examples of healthy personal boundaries

Intellectual boundaries:
- I will not allow anyone to dismiss or criticize my respectfully expressed thoughts and opinions.
- I will not allow anyone to make me feel like I have to justify my thoughts and opinions.
- I will let other people know if they have offended me in a respectful manner.

Spiritual boundaries:
- I will not allow anyone to make me feel guilty for my spiritual beliefs.
- I will commit to at least 30 minutes of daily meditation to strengthen my spiritual beliefs.

Emotional boundaries:
- I will not tolerate anyone going through my personal or emotional information without my consent.
- I will not allow anyone to assume they know how I feel.
- I will not entertain questions that are not appropriate for the relationship that I am in with another person.

Social boundaries:
- I will not be pressured into forming friendships with people I do not want like, admire or respect.
- I will only attend the social events that I want to and feel that benefit me.
- I will not allow anyone to make me that I should justify my hobbies or other social activities that I partake in.

Physical boundaries:
- I will not allow anyone to come into my living space without my prior permission.
- I will not allow anyone to intrude within my personal bubble without prior permission.
- I will not allow anyone to touch my body without prior permission.

Time boundaries:
- I will not commit to the projects that overextend me to please other people.
- I will be the one to dictate how much time I spend at events and social commitments.

- I will commit to and force my hourly rate at work no matter the circumstances that my clients convey.

Sexual boundaries:
- I will not be pressured into engaging in unwanted sexual acts.
- I will not allow anyone to criticize my sexual preferences.
- I will not accept it if someone has lied about their sexual health history or the use of contraceptives.

Material boundaries:
- I will not be pressured into lending or giving away my possessions.
- I will not give anyone authority over my major possession without council from my legal adviser.

I want to remind you that these personal boundaries not only serve to convey how you would like to be treated, but are a guideline as to how you treat other people.

Now that you have created these boundaries, you need to understand that enforcement is even more important because these words mean nothing if you are not willing to back them. When entering relationships, you need to clearly state what your boundaries are and the consequences of the other person overstepping the boundaries. To practice, you can start small. For example, if a waiter brought you the wrong order, kindly but assertively ask that you get what you actually ordered.

As you begin to get more comfortable with staking your boundaries, you will find that a habit develops whereby you clearly communicate what you need out of a relationship to maintain your self-worth and self-esteem. Continually practice so that this becomes an instinctive action rather than one that needs to be thought out and planned.

If someone has continually overstepped the boundaries, even after you have clearly communicated your discomfort, then you need to follow through with the consequences of this overstepping. That consequence may be seizing contact with that person. Having no contact with someone who continually overstepped your boundaries is nothing to feel guilty about. If anyone should feel guilty, it is the person who continually overstepped. Your self-worth and self-esteem will skyrocket once you learn to step up for yourself.

The four techniques listed above are powerful beyond belief when they used in the right way. They will surely help you reclaim your life after having it held under lock and key by a narcissist.

Chapter 5

How to Heal from the Emotional Trauma

Reinvent yourself

This book is not about telling you that you can return to the person you used to be. That is impossible because you have gone through an experience that has changed you on a fundamental level. Do not view that change as an evil. Everything and everyone changes. Every person that you meet and every event that you experience changes you.

Pain and trauma are two of the most powerful forces that demand change. The natural inclination is to bury pain or to pretend it does not exist because it is a hard truth to deal with and even harder to recover from.

So no, you never be the person that you were before. But you can be better. This chapter is dedicated to showing you how you can use this painful experience at the hand of a narcissistic man to grow and thrive. Here are a few powerful techniques you can use to lead you to recovery and develop into the magnificent creature you can be.

The only way that you can start on the road to recovery and healing is to first acknowledge that there is indeed pain and this period has made a change within you. Only then you can educate yourself on the ways to get in beyond that trauma so that you can live happily, healthily, and fully. In the following section of this chapter, we will discuss PTSD and how you may be a sufferer of it without knowing it.

What is PTSD?

PTSD stands for post-traumatic stress disorder and it is a mistaken assumption that it only affects soldiers and war veterans. PTSD is a mental disorder that arises after a person has experienced a traumatic event that involved the threat of injury or death. That threat may have been real or perceived by that person. By that definition, anyone who has experienced:

- Warlike conditions,
- A severe natural disaster such as an earthquake,
- Been involved in an accident or,
- Having been abused or assaulted in some manner, can develop PTSD symptoms.

On a day-to-day basis, we all experience things that cause stress. Stress, which is a response to a major challenge or something we perceive as a threat, releases chemicals and hormones in the body. The alterations of these chemicals and hormones trigger the flight-or-fight response in a person.

When a person is in fight-or-flight mode, they experience symptoms such as:

- Increased heartbeat.
- Increased breathing rate.
- Contracted blood vessels, which directs blood flow to muscles, which then allows quicker physical responses.
- The facilitated easier use of glucose by the muscles that use the energy needed for quicker physical responses.
- Increased perspiration.

Of course, these reactions and the release of hormones such as cortisol and adrenaline, are helpful in situations where we are in danger. Unfortunately, with persons who suffer from PTSD, the natural fight-or-flight response becomes altered by the traumatic event, which makes them feel stressed even in situations where they are safe.

Even though there is no one specific test to diagnose PTSD, only a licensed medical health professional can diagnose PTSD. Therefore, I advised that if you experience the symptoms that will be discussed below, please visit your doctor or find a licensed therapist to speak to.

The Signs and Symptoms of PTSD

PTSD symptoms can be mild but can often be disruptive of normal day-to-day activity because any sound, scent, taste, sight or touch can trigger them and therefore affect the sufferer's ability to function. PTSD symptoms fall into four categories. These categories are:

Intrusion

These symptoms can make it hard to function on a day-to-day basis as they are highly intrusive as the name suggests. The episodes of these symptoms are involuntary and many persons who suffer from them describe them as been thrown back into the traumatizing experience. These symptoms feel like the sufferer is reliving or re-experiencing the event.

The symptoms that fall into this category include:

- Having frequent nightmares about the traumatic event.
- Often experiencing vivid memories about the traumatic event.
- Having frequent flashbacks that relieve the event.
- Having severe mental distress when thinking about the event that caused PTSD symptoms and often largely experiencing associated physical distress.
- Experiencing psychological distress that is referred to as body cues or body memory.

Avoidance

These symptoms manifest themselves by the PTSD sufferer avoiding places, situations, and people that remind them of the traumatic event that triggered PTSD development. While this is quite understandable that a person might want to avoid triggers, this may lead to a lowered quality of life as this person may also avoid things that used to bring them joy. This can also lead to the person socially isolating themselves. Avoidance is not an effective tactic as not all situations can be avoided and no one can predict what person or situation can be a trigger.

Cognitive and emotional
These symptoms manifest themselves by affecting the person's mental processing of thoughts and their moods. They include:

- Having negative self-image and negative thoughts about one's self.
- Having trouble remembering important events that surrounded the main event that triggered PTSD development.
- Having reduced interest in activities that the sufferer once loved to participate in.
- Having intense yet distorted feelings of blame, guilt, and worry about the event.

Arousal and reactivity
This cluster of symptoms is also known as hyperarousal. They occur when a body suddenly becomes placed on high alert due to them rethinking or relieving the traumatic event. The body will act as if it is in danger even though there is no clear and present danger.

The symptoms in this category include:

- Being highly irritable and prone to bouts of anger.
- Being easily startled and having an exaggerated response being startled.
- Feeling constantly on edge are in a state of anxiety.
- Having trouble concentrating.
- Taking up self-destructive habits such as excessive drinking or drug use.

Hyperarousal symptoms are often accompanied by a number state of emotion, avoidance behavior and having flashbacks of the traumatic event.

Being Diagnosed with PTSD

To become diagnosed with PTSD, a person must experience the following symptoms for one month or longer:

- Two or more cognitive and mood symptoms.
- One or more avoidance symptoms.
- Two or more arousal and reactivity symptoms.
- One or more intrusion symptom.

How Victims of Narcissistic Abuse Develop PTSD

Even though PTSD is often called shell shock or battle fatigue due to its close association with war veterans, which is largely a male-dominated area, women are 2 times more likely to be diagnosed with PTSD. Women are also more likely to suffer from symptoms longer and typically wait an average of 4 years to seek professional help deal with PTSD compared to men, who usually seek help within one year of seeing symptoms.

Symptoms that women experience are also slightly more exaggerated. As such, they are more likely to:

- Be easily startled.
- Be more sensitive to reminders on the trauma that caused PTSD.
- Develop other mental disorders associated with PTSD like anxiety and depression.
- Closet their emotions and, therefore, be plagued with feelings of numbness.

Many people are under the mistaken assumption that PTSD needs to develop from severe physical abuse when is related to relationships but that is not true. Violence can also take on a psychological form, which it often does as a narcissist often employs tools like verbal and emotional abuse, sabotage, gaslighting, manipulation, lies, and ridicule. Being chronically exposed to such abuse can make a person develop PTSD.

This particularly develops because the narcissist can warp reality to suit their own purpose as exampled by engaging in love-bombing after abusive incidents. They are such skilled manipulators that they can even sometimes convinced the victim that the victim is the abuser.

Even if you experienced narcissistic abuse years before, it is important to consider the idea that you might suffer from PTSD. Even if you have not experienced symptoms for a long time, anything can trigger symptoms without a moment's notice. As a result, PTSD symptoms can appear at any time and often leave the victim re-experiencing the traumatic event as if it is the first time.

It is never too late to get treatment for PTSD even if you have forgotten the specific details of the trauma. This is specifically helpful to know for victims of narcissistic abuse who do not even realize that they were being abused and, therefore, likely buried the events of the trauma. This needs to be done with the help of a trained professional as this person will guide the victim into digging into the past trauma in a safe way.

Why Healing from Trauma or PTSD Triggered by Narcissistic Abuse Is Different

A victim of this kind of abuse often wonders why she lives like this while others live in relative peace. This thought process can lead to the person believing that the fault lies within them or else this abuse would not have occurred or continued. Often persons who develop PTSD from accidents or other isolated in the incidences do not take on this type of thinking. These events can be seen as a random incident that no one has control over. PTSD sufferers that are victims of narcissistic abuse typically blame themselves for the abuse that they suffered. As a result, this person needs to work on their psyche and sense of smell to get over the abuse and PTSD symptoms.

This is supported by the behavior of the narcissist because this person always has to play the victim even though he is the one who treats you terribly. Lies and manipulation will be used to make the victim blame herself instead. This will make you feel worthless, like you cannot do anything right and that no one else can enjoy your company since it seems to be so terrible.

Recovery from this is terribly hard, but it is one that can be made with a choice. You have to make the choice to stop constantly living in a state of fight or flight. You have to make a choice that you will let go of the betrayal and emotional abuse that this person inflicted upon you. You have to make the choice to stop letting the pain control your life.

You have to also realize that this is a process that takes time and will not happen overnight nor do the memories completely disappear. There will be times when you have symptoms often and expectedly. There will likely be times when you revisit the trauma that this person inflicted upon you. Making the choice does not mean that your life will change instantly. Making this choice means that you will do what is necessary to put this incident in the past so that you could look forward to a brighter future.

Below you will find some techniques for finally putting that part of your life in the past where it belongs. These techniques can be employed even if you do not suffer from PTSD symptoms but still need to heal from the trauma inflicted by narcissistic abuse at the hands of the person you trusted to be your life partner.

Healing from Trauma or PTSD from Narcissistic Abuse

Get the Support You Need

Healing and recovering from any sort of trauma is always easier with help. Going at healing alone can often leave the victim feeling stuck, especially if she plagued by painful memories or a constant sense of danger. Also, PTSD commonly makes sufferers feel disconnected from other people, which tends to lead to social isolation and withdrawing from activities where other people are involved. However, it is important to stay connected with human life and with the people that care about you.

If you have a trusted friend or family member who will allow you to talk and listen without judgement, that is a great option.

Other options that provide support in this time of need include joining a support group where you can gain guidance from a licensed professional that has experience in dealing abuse and trauma. This will also allow you to socialize with other persons who have gone through similar challenges. Developing a bond with such people will allow you to feel not so alone.

Also, do not be afraid to reach out and seek professional help, especially if you find yourself:

- Unable to sleep.
- Using addictive substances such as alcohol and drugs to cope.

- Lacking the energy to carry out your daily responsibilities.
- Often feeling anxious or fearful.
- Experiencing depression.
- Avoiding social situations.
- Having nightmares and flashbacks often.
- Experience suicidal thoughts.

If you experience these severe symptoms, then this mental health professional will help guide you into practicing behavioral therapy, which is a type of therapy that addresses the umbrella group of mental health disorders. This type of therapy helps the victim to change behaviors that may be unhealthy or self-destructive.

Get Active

Exercise promotes the release of special chemicals in the body known as endorphins. These chemicals react with receptors in the brain that reduce a person's perception of pain and negative emotions. Many people describe the feeling after a workout as euphoric and it is sometimes known as a runner's high because it promotes a positive and energized outlook on life.

Endorphins also act as a sedative and make it easier to fall asleep faster and stay asleep longer. Apart from improving sleep quality, alleviating pain and improving mood, exercising helps reduce the likelihood of developing medical health issues like depression and anxiety, reduce stress levels, and boost self-esteem.

Added benefits of exercising include:

- Strengthening the heart.
- Lowering blood pressure.
- Increasing strength.
- Improving muscle tone.
- Strengthening bones.
- Reducing body fat.
- Increasing energy levels.

Because there is movement involved in exercising, it can help a person suffering from PTSD or trauma from narcissistic abuse feel unstuck. This helps the person think clearer, so that they can strategize and develop a plan for moving forward in a more positive and uplifting direction.

Examples of exercises that help include:

- Walking.
- Running.
- Jogging.
- Low-impact aerobics like cycling and Nordic walking.
- Dancing.
- Biking.
- Tennis.
- Swimming.

While the exercises listed above are specifically mentioned, any form of physical activity and exercise can help. It might also be helpful to join an exercise group or class so that you can socialize and get the added benefit of getting out of the house and out of your comfort zone.

A helpful tip to gain the most benefit from exercising, especially when doing an activity such as walking, running, and dancing, is to focus on how your body feels rather than your thoughts. While you do more strenuous activities such as rock climbing, martial arts, or weight training, focus on the movement of your body. Not only is this tip helpful to ensure that you do not get hurt, but again, this also takes you out of your head and into a different zone that is free of the trauma that you experienced.

Eat Right

Food is a basic necessity that facilitates human life and living. As a result, many people eat without realizing the impact that their diet has on their general health and wellness. Being alive is not enough. You need to eat well to ensure that you feel your best and perform your best every day.

A diet also has a huge impact on your mental and emotional health. Therefore, it is important that someone who has suffered trauma or PTSD be aware and mindful of what they eat as an unbalanced and innutritious diet can promote the flare up of symptoms of PTSD and trauma.

Here are a few tips for getting the most out of your diet to help treat your PTSD and trauma-related symptoms:

- Eat breakfast every day so that your brain is better equipped to deal with the challenges faced

throughout that day. This also keeps your energy up.
- Eat balanced meals throughout the day to keep your energy up.
- Avoid skipping meals.
- Avoid using addictive substances such as alcohol and drugs.
- Consume omega-3 fatty acids. Fatty fish, nuts and seeds are omega-3 fatty acid-rich foods. Omega-3 fatty acids help promote good emotional health.
- Limit the consumption of refined grains, sugars, fried foods, and processed foods as they can cause mood swings and fluctuations in your energy.
- Do not stress eat. Stress eating can include binge eating and eating without thinking because you feel stressed. This can lead to a host of physical health problems such as unhealthy weight gains and an increased risk of developing cardiovascular diseases. Instead, develop healthier coping mechanisms such as planning your meals and seeking emotional support so that you do not overeat in times of stress.

Get Social

Social isolation may have been a technique that the narcissist employed to keep you under his control. You may have also socially isolated yourself as a way of coping. However, it is a lot easier to heal with friends and family who care about you are surrounding you. Even hanging out with acquaintances who do not know about your problems can help ease the struggle and boost your mood.

To help ease out of social isolation, you can:

- Start a new hobby or join a class or club where you can meet new people.
- Start accepting invitations to parties and other social events more often even if you feel like you should stay at home.
- Call up an old friend you have not spoken to in a while just to get reacquainted.
- Invite a friend or family member out to simple activities like watching a movie or catching a bite to eat.

Getting back into the act of socializing after spending a long time socially isolated can be hard to do, but the key is to take baby steps and to be consistent.

Make Quality Sleep a Priority
Getting an adequate amount of sleep is as important as eating right and exercising regularly. It is great for the development of good mental and emotional health, which is clearly a plus if you suffer from PTSD or trauma.

Unfortunately, suffering from abuse at a narcissistic partner's hand can make it difficult to get a good night's sleep even long after the abuse has ended. Here are a few tips you can employ to increase the likelihood that you will get the amount of and quality of sleep that you need on a daily basis:

- Engage in relaxing activities such as reading or having a warm bath at least an hour before bedtime.
- Do not eat heavy meals at least 2 hours before bedtime.
- Even though engaging in exercise can help promote getting quality sleep, you should not engage in it a few hours before bedtime.
- Do not expose yourself to blue light such as the light emitted from smartphones and computers at least 30 minutes before bedtime.
- Sleep in a dark, cool and quiet room.
- Ensure that your sleeping arrangements are comfortable and inviting.
- Do not use your bedroom for any other activity apart from sleeping.
- Make it a goal to receive between 7 and 8 hours of sleep every night.
- Develop a bedtime and morning routine so that you wake up and go to bed at the same time every day.

Employ Relaxation Techniques
Employing relaxation techniques is meant to slow down your breathing and heart rate, lower your blood pressure, bring your mind and body into a state of balance, and lower your stress levels. This cannot be done by just sitting down in front of the television. You need to employ specific relaxation techniques such as meditation, yoga, deep breathing, and Tai chi.

Because it is such an unconscious activity, not many people realize the deep impact of breathing and breathing correctly has on everyday living. Not only does breathing correctly, which means allowing your breath to move your abdomen rather than your chest, have physical benefits, it also has emotional and mental health benefits. It can be combined with specified music and aromatherapy.

A simple deep breathing exercise includes the following steps:

- Sit with your back straight in a quiet, cool area and place your hands on your thighs.
- Breathe in through your nose, ensuring that your stomach rises with the motion.
- Exhale through your mouth, ensuring that your stomach moves with the motion.

Repeat this as many times as you need while focusing on the rise and fall of your stomach and the movement of air in and out of your lungs.

There are several types of meditation that you can employ to achieve a state of relaxation. Examples include mindful meditation and body scan meditation.

Both yoga and tai chi employ body movements and stationary poses that are combined with deep breathing to reduce stress and anxiety as well as improve balance stamina flexibility and strength.

No matter what type of relaxation technique that you employ, it is important that you set time in your daily schedule so that you develop a habit that promotes the good health of your mind and heart.

More Activities That Promote Healing from Trauma and PTSD from Narcissistic Abuse

These include:

- Spending time in nature. Being outdoors promotes relaxation and gaining peace by being away from the fast pace of urban life. You can participate in activities like hiking, camping, and skiing, all of which are nature-themed activities to help soothe PTSD symptoms as well as transitioning into recovery from narcissistic abuse.
- Practice aromatherapy. Aromatherapy is a holistic healing treatment that has ancient roots. It utilizes natural plant extract to promote better health and well-being. These plant extracts often come in the form of essential oils. Essential oils that are great for reducing stress and anxiety include jasmine, lavender, clary sage, German chamomile, bergamot, rose, and ylang-ylang.
- Get professional massages. Massages use strokes of the hands and fingers to relieve muscle tension. This relief can extend to your mental and emotional health. Therefore, I highly recommend that you partake in this activity if you can afford to do so.
- Take up a cause. Volunteer in some way to your community such as feeding the homeless. Not only will this incite feelings of gratefulness, it will also

take your focus of your own mental and emotional distress and place it on giving back.

Chapter 6

Discover Your True Worth

Your self-esteem and self-worth are the value that you placed upon yourself. They are a reflection of whether or not you like yourself. They reflect whether and not you feel that you deserve to be happy and whether or not you show yourself kindness and compassion. They reflect whether or not you are comfortable with your strengths and are aware of the positive things that make you, "You." Your self-worth and self-esteem, tell everyone whether or not you believe that you as an individual matter.

Your narcissistic former partner did a number on you, so it is understandable if your self-esteem and self-worth are not up to par with what they should be. The first step in rectifying that is becoming more self-aware. You need to have a baseline for what you generally feel about yourself so that you can then use that as a guideline to move forward and increase your self-esteem and self-worth accordingly. Education is your best friend.

Self-esteem and self-worth are not the same things, although they might be described as flip sides of the same coin. While your self-esteem is a general gauge for what you think, believe and feel about yourself, your self-worth is recognizing that you can be even greater than these things. High self-worth comes from recognizing that you are lovable, that you are a necessary component to this life and that your value is beyond measure. In simple terms, self-esteem speaks to you *thinking* that you are lovable, necessary, and valuable but not necessarily believing this while self-worth is having that absolute conviction of the fact. As a result, having high self-esteem does not equate to having a high sense of self-worth. But on the other hand, if you have a high sense of self-worth, you will have a high sense of self-esteem. This chapter is dedicated to making you *know* on a fundamental level that you are lovable, precious, and special.

Having low self-esteem and feelings of self-worth is characterized by having a general feeling of unease about yourself, which leads to lacking confidence in yourself and your abilities on a fundamental level. Not only does a person with low self-worth suffer from low self-confidence, but other characteristics include:

- Suffering from mental health illnesses such as depression and anxiety.
- Having difficulty accepting compliments.

- Suffering from feelings of inadequacy.
- Having a propensity to socially isolate one's self.
- Having low expectations of one's self.
- Placing the needs of other people ahead of one's own.
- Neglecting one's emotional needs.
- Having difficulty listening to one's intuition.
- Being overly concerned with the thoughts and opinions of other people about one's self.

Luckily, if you are currently suffering from low self-worth and self-esteem, you are not stuck in this condition forever. There are things that you can do to build your sense of self-worth. Below you will find 5 such measures.

Talk to Yourself Kindly

You may not have realized it, but the voice of the narcissist that you lived with for so long may have become your internal voice. Of course, this voice is constantly criticizing you and dismissing your needs as fickle things.

The internal dialogue that goes on in your head is known as self-talk. You may not realize it yet, but you have the power to influence what is said because this talk is influenced by your thoughts, ideas, beliefs, and things that you are unsure about. These thoughts, ideas and others center on your perception of the world around you, other people and yourself.

This is why self-talk has the power to be both negative and positive. As a result, if you have a negative outlook on life and yourself, your self-talk will predominantly be negative. On the other hand, if you have a more optimistic outlook and personality then this self-talk will be more positive and hopeful.

Self-talk can be influenced by your current level of self-esteem and self-worth. On the other hand, you can increase your sense of self-esteem and self-worth by practicing more positive self-talk. There are other benefits to steering your internal dialogue toward a more positive outlook and they include:

- Enhancing your general performance and well-being.
- Having a greater sense of satisfaction with your life.
- Improving cardiovascular health.
- Boosting immune system function.
- Aiding in alleviating pain.
- Increasing vitality.
- Decreasing the incidence of developing mental health diseases like depression and anxiety.

Even though practicing positive self-talk has so many great benefits, our instinctive human reaction is to practice negative self-talk. This is an evolutionary trait that was used in the time of our ancestors to up the rate of survival. Having a pessimistic view allowed cavemen to better predict the worst-case scenario so that they could be prepared. Even though this practice is not necessary for survival in most cases in modern society, it is still something that persists in the human psyche.

Therefore, to beat this natural human inclination and circumstances that promote it, you must first be aware of what it is and how it happens. Negative self-talk falls into one of four categories. They are:

- **Catastrophizing.** These types of negative thoughts make the person expect the worst at all times even going so far as to defy logic in the expectation.
- **Personalizing**. These types of negative thoughts make a person blame themselves for everything that happens even if the circumstances are far out of their reach to control.
- **Magnifying.** These types of negative thoughts make a person focus on the negative aspects of a situation while blatantly ignoring any and all positives that came out of that situation.
- **Polarizing.** These types of thoughts take on an either-or approach. Things are only good or bad, or black or white. There is no middle ground and as such, thoughts tend to favor the black or bad.

Now that you are aware of the type of negative thoughts that can persist in your mind, you can then learn to switch them around so that they are more positive. This is a practice that takes a conscious effort on your part to monitor what type of talk goes on in your head.

Let us practice with a few examples.

Your negative thought may be, *I have failed and so, will be a failure forever*. You can switch that negative self-talk and practice a more positive outlook by instead thinking something like, *I am proud of my effort because it took much courage to go outside of my comfort zone.*

Another negative thought may take a form like, *I am out of shape and should not bother trying to achieve my ideal weight.* A positive thought to counter that may be, *I am capable and persistent and will do what is necessary to ensure that I become as healthy as can be.*

Practicing positive self-talk is another process that does not happen overnight. You have to be persistent and consistent with it to see results. This will allow you to develop a new habit whereby your natural inclination is to take on a positive outlook on the world and yourself. That positive outlook will help boost your sense of self-esteem and self-worth. Tips you can employ to do this include:

- **Identifying things that trigger negative self-talk.** For example, your work life may be a circumstance where you experience a lot of negative self-talk. Identify what about that situation trigger those thoughts, so that you can mentally prepare yourself to counter these thoughts with positive self-talk.
- **Stop and evaluate how you feel often.** Do this especially when you feel down as this is a time where negative thoughts are likely to manifest.
- **Surround yourself with positive people.** It is unfortunate to say, but you are the company that you keep. Therefore, if you find yourself hanging around people that are perpetually negative, then your internal dialogue will take on that energy. Actively choose the type of energy that you absorb and hang out with people who promote positive vibes and interactions.
- **Learn to use humor to counter negative self-talk.** Humor allows a person to feel lighter and less stressed and therefore, less likely to give in to negative self-talk.
- **Use positive affirmations.** These statements boost the likelihood that you will take on a more positive outlook and therefore, use positive self-talk to communicate with yourself.

You are now the one in control of your thoughts. Taken even that power away from the narcissist and replace his voice with one the uplifts and empowers you.

Work on Your Self-Image

Your self-image is what you believe about your personality, appearance, and abilities. The narcissist would have taken punches at your self-image as well to suit his purpose of manipulating and controlling you. He would have made you see your physical appearance, your capabilities and your personality through a lens of his making. This is your wake-up call to look at yourself through a new lens. The best way to cultivate that new lens is to first work on acknowledging the things that you are good at.

Next, if there are things about your personality that you do not like, acknowledge what they are and work on changing them. Personality is a fluid thing. You can change it anytime. You have seen how being in the presence of the narcissist can change your personality for the worst. Now you can work on changing it for the best. One of the surest ways to do this is by changes bad habits that you may have such as being abrasive. Taking on more positive personality traits like being more kind and honest goes a long way in boosting self-image.

One of the hardest-hitting contributing factors for poor self-image is body image. Weight, how we dress, our facial features... All of it and more play a part in how we feel about ourselves. Again, this is something that you can take control of. You need to learn to feel comfortable in your own skin and to see the beauty in you. Beauty is not just skin deep. It is about how you carry yourself, how accepting you are of yourself and how open you are to the fact that you are a beautiful person. Beauty is not a state of body. It is a state of mind.

Things you can do to promote a more positive body image include:

- **Celebrating and appreciating all the things that your body can do**. You can run. You can dance. You can breathe. You exist... All of these things make you special and beautiful no matter how simple or common they are.
- **When you need reminding, make a list of the top 10 things that you like about yourself.** Read this list often and place it in an area where it is easily visible and accessible to you. This frequent reminder of your likeable traits solidifies the facts in your mind and therefore, boosts your sense of self-worth.
- **Turn negative self-talk about your body image into positive self-talk.**
- **Wear clothes that make you feel comfortable and good about your body**. Do not try to fit into the social norm. Work with your own body shape, size and your own needs, not against them to fit in with the current trend.
- **Do not allow yourself to be fooled by mass media and social media messages about you what you should be or look like.** What you are is beautiful and there is no need to change to fit into a mold.
- **Take the time to do something nice for yourself often**. It can be as simple as taking a nap

when you need it or as extravagant as going on vacation to an exotic location to restore your focus and energy. The point is to boost your mental and emotional environment so that your whole person feels good and cared for.

Be Proud of the Fact That You Are a Survivor of Narcissistic Abuse

This narcissist tried to break you, but just from reading this book I know that you are not broken, merely cracked. A crack can be mended and be transformed into something truly beautiful and inspiring as exampled by you.

Not many people can go through the things that you have gone through and still make it out on top. You are strong and resilient and both of these traits deserve to be celebrated and appreciated, especially by you. Not only have you survived this abuse and taken steps to get out of the vicious cycle, but you have also taken steps to make a bigger, better, brighter future for yourself. That takes guts and you have got the stuff to make that happen.

So celebrate the fact that you have gone through this and you have left that situation to ensure that your future is not the dismal existence that your narcissistic ex wanted to be. You are such a strong being that you have taken that power back from him.

Now is the time to focus on your goals. With every goal that you tick off your list, you will feel a notch been placed on your self-worth and self-esteem. You will realize that you've got this and that you will make it work despite circumstances that try to bring you down.

Focus on the change that you would like to make in your life and how you would like to go. As you manifest that change, you will notice the increased positivity in your mental, emotional and spiritual environment.

Use the Power of Visualization

The mind is a powerful thing. It has the power to manifest the things that you can visualize even if you are not aware of it. Use that power to your advantage. See yourself as self-confident, highly esteemed and a person with self-worth that is through the roof. Visualize that person often.

Notice how she looks, how she talks, her body language, how she enforces her personal boundaries, etc. Think about it just before you go to sleep and first thing in the morning. Think about her when you are having a bad day and your self-worth has taken a hit. Picture her in your mind's eye after when you have taken a won in upping your self-confidence. Do not lose sight of her no matter what happens.

Give her a name. Call her future [insert your name here]. And you know what will happen after you have done all these things? One day, maybe even without your knowledge, you will be that woman with a high sense of self-esteem and self-worth.

Do not dismiss this as here say or magical nonsense. Seeing is believing and if you bombard your brain with the visualization enough, you will automatically take steps to ensure that this is the outcome that you gain. This visualization gives you something to work toward and motivates you to keep on working even through the tough times. Visualization works because it activates neurons in our brains that generate impulses to perform real-life action. So you see, obtaining the self-worth you should have will not be a magical or easy process, but it will be possible through your own manifestation.

Start Acknowledging and Celebrating Your Accomplishments

Most people focused on the things that they have not accomplished yet and forget to be grateful and appreciative of the things that they have already done. We often get consumed by doing and doing and forget to take a moment and focus much-needed attention on the fruits of our hard work. This is especially true for abuse survivors such as the victims of narcissistic abuse who have had their accomplishments swept under the rug by their narcissistic partner. Acknowledging and celebrating your accomplishments is a form of self-care that goes a long way in boosting your morale. It not only increases self-esteem and self-worth, but it also serves as motivation to keep on going and accomplishing even more.

You do not have to keep your success in accomplishing your goals and dreams to yourself either. You can express it without sounding like a narcissist or a braggart. You need to learn to be comfortable with the fact that you have made great strides in not only removing yourself from a toxic situation but overcoming in a big and bright way. You are greatness personified. Do not feel awkward in expressing that. You do not brag about it. You simply state it.

In the same breath, that I say acknowledge and celebrate your accomplishments, I also say do not allow yourself to be defined by them. I say this for two reasons. The first reason is that you are meant for bigger and better things. So while it is great to stop periodically and marvel at what you have accomplished, you should also know when it is time to get back on track to thriving and growing.

The second reason is that there will be times where you are not successful in accomplishing what you set out to do. Ensure that your self-esteem and self-worth are not tied to those tasks. There are more and should remain on an upward trend whether or not you accomplish a goal. The key here is to learn to be educated by disappointments so that in the end they do not seem like failures but instead, lessons that catapult you be better things.

Conclusion

In conclusion of this book, I would like to talk about forgiveness. About forgiving your narcissistic ex-partner and forgiving yourself. Forgiveness is not something that you should give lightly. Rather, it is a tool that you must use to make peace with the past because it is necessary so that you gain the tools of empathy, kindness, understanding, and compassion needed to move forward with your future.

Forgive but Never Forget

You do not need the narcissist's consent to forgive. In fact, forgiving the narcissist (if you choose to do so) is not for his purpose. Rather, it is for your sense of well-being and peace of mind. This is a choice that you make of your own free will without any influence from him. This person does not even need to know that you have taken on the venture to forgive his behavior and attitudes towards you.

However, forgiving the narcissist pales in comparison to working on forgiving yourself. You placed a lot of guilt and blame on yourself for being in that relationship with the narcissist. This may have been promoted by the narcissist or something you naturally took on as time went by. More than likely, you placed the blame on yourself after this relationship as well. The reasons that victims of narcissist relationship assigned themselves blame are wide and varied.

They feel guilty for not seeing past the narcissist's lies. They blame themselves for not leaving sooner. They blame themselves for not taking the advice of their loved ones and families. They blame themselves for the entire relationship and everything that happened before, during and after. What I want you to realize is that the blame that you placed on yourself is blown completely out of proportion. Of course, no one is completely blameless in the ending of a relationship. However, the burden that you are carrying must be let go because it is unfounded and unnecessary for you to continue to punish yourself in this way.

Forgiving, especially yourself, is a hard task to do. It is also an elusive thing because while you may feel that you have gotten past the blame game today, tomorrow it might be another story. But no matter how elusive it is, you must keep pursuing it so that you protect your general health and wellness as well as your spirit.

The forgiveness of yourself is also needed so that you can eventually develop a romantic relationship sustained by a healthy bond and connection with another man in the future. You have not been sentenced to a life of loneliness and singularity because of this failed relationship with a narcissist. You know what a healthy relationship is not because of what you have gone through with the narcissist so you can avoid having to go through that experience again.

While most people enter a romantic relationship to find love, compatibility, and security, the narcissist only came to cover up his all low self-esteem and self-worth issues. This person has never genuinely been concerned about your feelings. That is a hard pill to swallow, but swallow it you must. This person came to take from you and while you may have been fooled in the beginning, you now know the true face of this person. You now know that this person came to tear down your self-esteem, self-confidence, and self-worth so that they can feel a sense of fulfillment in their own poorly nourished sense of self. This person wanted the spotlight and they took it by force.

This hurts you, of course, but it is now time to sever the bond that you had with this person so that you can finally thrive. It is time that you let go of the past so that you can shine in the way that you were meant to today and tomorrow. That was a painful chapter that you went through, but it is behind you now. You have the power to write the future in words that you choose. Change is happening. Embrace it as a good thing. Take new chances so that you can learn and grow. Become the powerful, resilient, and blessed woman that I know you are and you will discover in time through your own effort and hard work.

Final Thoughts

My last words include a big thank you for downloading this book. Every word was carefully considered to help you get through this difficult time in your life. These words were written to show you the value in yourself as a woman and as a person. They were written to show you that you deserve to be loved and desired in an uplifting and empowering way by your romantic partner. They were written to show you that you are a survivor and the blame for your marriage ending this way rests squarely on the narcissist's shoulders.

This book was also written to show you that you are not alone, even though you might feel that way. There are many other women like you and many other people like me willing to provide support to help you regain your power.

You have embarked on a journey of self-discovery after a toxic relationship. All journeys that are worth having and that promote growth and development have potholes and are haunted by unexpected twists, turns, and surprises that will catch you off guard. But please, do enjoy every moment of your self-discovery journey. Allow yourself to feel every emotion that it has to offer and use the tips, tricks, and strategies provided by this book to help guide you through healing and recovery after your narcissistic relationship.

My hope is that you gain value from every page of this book and that you use the words inside to take a proactive approach to get behind the wheel of your life and steering the vehicle in the direction that you want it to go.

Good luck!

Isabel

Reference

Bailey J. A., 2nd (2003). The foundation of self-esteem. *Journal of the National Medical Association, 95*(5), 388–393.

Baskin-Sommers, A., Krusemark, E., & Ronningstam, E. (2014). Empathy in narcissistic personality disorder: from clinical and empirical perspectives. *Personality disorders, 5*(3), 323–333. **https://doi.org/10.1037/per0000061**

Bisson, J. I., Cosgrove, S., Lewis, C., & Robert, N. P. (2015). Post-traumatic stress disorder. *BMJ (Clinical research ed.), 351*, h6161. **https://doi.org/10.1136/bmj.h6161**

Brunell, A. B., Robison, J., Deems, N. P., & Okdie, B. M. (2018). Are narcissists more attracted to people in relationships than to people not in relationships?. *PloS one, 13*(3), e0194106.

https://doi.org/10.1371/journal.pone.0194106

Carlson, E. N., Vazire, S., & Oltmanns, T. F. (2011). You probably think this paper's about you: narcissists' perceptions of their personality and reputation. *Journal of personality and social psychology, 101*(1), 185–201.

https://doi.org/10.1037/a0023781

Charuvastra, A., & Cloitre, M. (2008). Social bonds and posttraumatic stress disorder. *Annual review of psychology, 59*, 301–328. **https://doi.org/10.1146/annurev.psych.58.110405.085650**

Di Pierro, R., Mattavelli, S., & Gallucci, M. (2016). Narcissistic Traits and Explicit Self-Esteem: The Moderating Role of Implicit Self-View. *Frontiers in psychology, 7*, 1815. **https://doi.org/10.3389/fpsyg.2016.01815**

Dunn, B. D., Billotti, D., Murphy, V., & Dalgleish, T. (2009). The consequences of effortful emotion regulation when processing distressing material: a comparison of suppression and acceptance. *Behaviour research and therapy, 47*(9), 761–773. **https://doi.org/10.1016/j.brat.2009.05.007**

Gabbard, G. O., & Crisp-Han, H. (2016). The many faces of narcissism. *World psychiatry : official journal of the World Psychiatric Association (WPA), 15*(2), 115–116. **https://doi.org/10.1002/wps.20323**

Gildersleeve M. (2012). Demystifying paradoxical characteristics of narcissistic personality disorder. *Indian journal of psychological medicine, 34*(4), 403–404. **https://doi.org/10.4103/0253-7176.108236**

Henriksen, I. O., Ranøyen, I., Indredavik, M. S., & Stenseng, F. (2017). The role of self-esteem in the development of psychiatric problems: a three-year prospective study in a clinical sample of adolescents. *Child and adolescent psychiatry and mental health, 11*, 68.

https://doi.org/10.1186/s13034-017-0207-y

Jauk, E., Weigle, E., Lehmann, K., Benedek, M., & Neubauer, A. C. (2017). The Relationship between Grandiose and Vulnerable (Hypersensitive) Narcissism. *Frontiers in psychology, 8*, 1600.

https://doi.org/10.3389/fpsyg.2017.01600

Kacel, E. L., Ennis, N., & Pereira, D. B. (2017). Narcissistic Personality Disorder in Clinical Health Psychology Practice: Case Studies of Comorbid Psychological Distress and Life-Limiting Illness. *Behavioral medicine (Washington, D.C.), 43*(3), 156–164.

https://doi.org/10.1080/08964289.2017.1301875

McLean J. (2007). Psychotherapy with a Narcissistic Patient Using Kohut's Self Psychology Model. *Psychiatry (Edgmont (Pa. : Township)), 4*(10), 40–47.

Miller, J. D., Campbell, W. K., & Pilkonis, P. A. (2007). Narcissistic personality disorder: relations with distress and functional impairment. *Comprehensive psychiatry, 48*(2), 170–177.

https://doi.org/10.1016/j.comppsych.2006.10.003

Olff M. (2012). Bonding after trauma: on the role of social support and the oxytocin system in traumatic stress. *European journal of psychotraumatology, 3*, 10.3402/ejpt.v3i0.18597. https://doi.org/10.3402/ejpt.v3i0.18597

Olff M. (2017). Sex and gender differences in post-traumatic stress disorder: an update. *European Journal of Psychotraumatology, 8*(sup4), 1351204. https://doi.org/10.1080/20008198.2017.1351204

Rogoza, R., Żemojtel-Piotrowska, M., Kwiatkowska, M. M., & Kwiatkowska, K. (2018). The Bright, the Dark, and the Blue Face of Narcissism: The Spectrum of Narcissism in Its Relations to the Metatraits of Personality, Self-Esteem, and the Nomological Network of Shyness, Loneliness, and Empathy. *Frontiers in psychology, 9*, 343. https://doi.org/10.3389/fpsyg.2018.00343

Simpson, J. A., & Steven Rholes, W. (2017). Adult Attachment, Stress, and Romantic Relationships. *Current opinion in psychology, 13*, 19–24.

https://doi.org/10.1016/j.copsyc.2016.04.006

Srivastava, S., Tamir, M., McGonigal, K. M., John, O. P., & Gross, J. J. (2009). The social costs of emotional suppression: a prospective study of the transition to college. *Journal of personality and social psychology, 96*(4), 883–897. https://doi.org/10.1037/a0014755

Stinson, F. S., Dawson, D. A., Goldstein, R. B., Chou, S. P., Huang, B., Smith, S. M., Ruan, W. J., Pulay, A. J., Saha, T. D., Pickering, R. P., & Grant, B. F. (2008). Prevalence, correlates, disability, and comorbidity of DSM-IV narcissistic personality disorder: results from the wave 2 national epidemiologic survey on alcohol and related conditions. *The Journal of clinical psychiatry, 69*(7), 1033–1045.

https://doi.org/10.4088/jcp.v69n0701

Wright, A., Stepp, S. D., Scott, L. N., Hallquist, M. N., Beeney, J. E., Lazarus, S. A., & Pilkonis, P. A. (2017). The effect of pathological narcissism on interpersonal and affective processes in social interactions. *Journal of abnormal psychology, 126*(7), 898–910.

https://doi.org/10.1037/abn0000286

More Books by the Author

"**Narcissistic Mothers**" Recover your Life from Toxic Family Relationships. A Healing Guide for Understanding Narcissism and Manipulation. Heal Yourself from Emotional Abuse and Learn Your Really Worth.

"**Narcissist Partner Abuse**" - Stop Being a Narcissism Victim. Complete Guide to Get your Personal Power Back and to Recover from a Relationship with a Toxic Manipulative Partner with Personality Disorder.

Made in the USA
Columbia, SC
17 September 2020